THE
COMPLETE
SEWING MACHINE
HANDBOOK

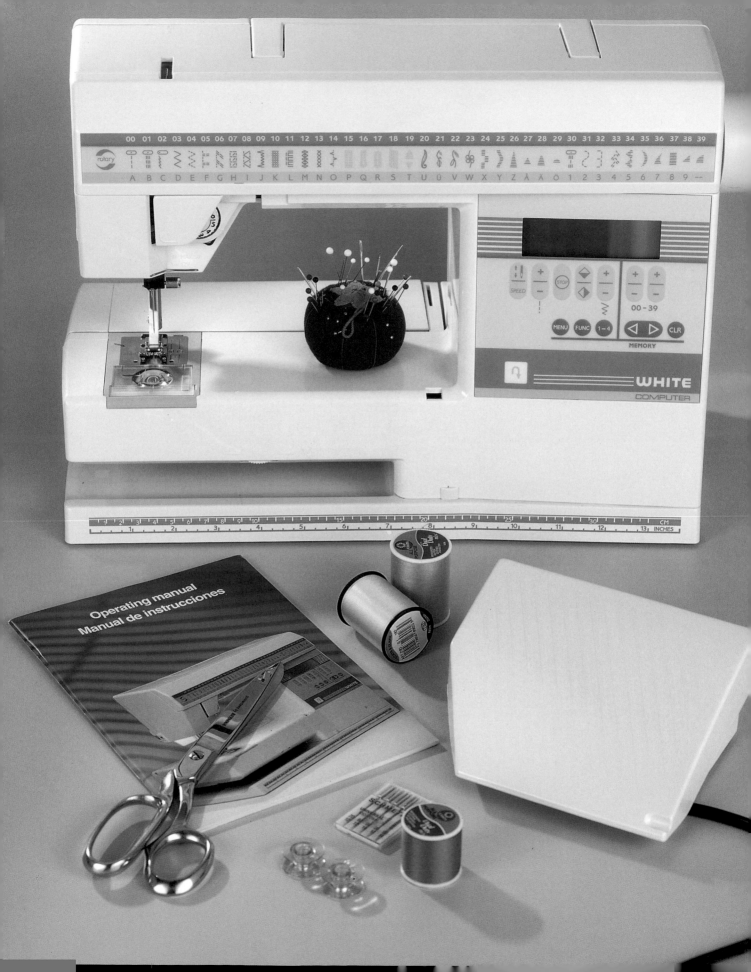

THE
COMPLETE
SEWING MACHINE
HANDBOOK

By Karen E. Kunkel

Sterling Publishing Co., Inc.
New York

A Sterling/Sewing Information Resources Book

Sewing Information Resources

Owner: JoAnn Pugh-Gannon
Photography: Kaz Ayukawa, K Graphics
Book Design and Page Layout: Rose Sheifer, Graphic Productions
Index: Anne Leach
Copy Edit: Mary Helen Schiltz

Sewing Information Resources is a registered trademark of GANZ Inc.

Library of Congress Cataloging-in-Publication Data

Kunkel, Karen E.
      The complete sewing machine handbook / by Karen E. Kunkel.
         p.   cm.
      "A Sterling/sewing information resources book."
      Includes bibliographical references and index.
      ISBN 0-8069-0848-3
        1. Machine sewing. 2. Sewing machines. I. Title.
  TT713.K86   1997
  646.2'044—dc21   97-41176
                                                    CIP

A Sterling/Sewing Information Resources Book

2 4 6 8 10 9 7 5 3 1

Published by Sterling Publishing Company, Inc.
387 Park Avenue South, New York, N.Y. 10016
Produced by Sewing Information Resources
P.O. Box 330, Wasco, Il. 60183
©1997 by Karen Kunkel
Distributed in Canada by Sterling Publishing
c/o Canadian Manda Group, One Atlantic Avenue, Suite 105
Toronto, Ontario, Canada, N6K 3E7
Distributed in Great Britain and Europe by Cassell PLC
Wellington House, 125 Strand, London WC2R 0BB, England
Distributed in Australia by Capricorn Link (Australia) Pty Ltd.
P.O. Box 6651, Baulkham Hills, Business Centre, NSW 2153, Australia
Printed in Hong Kong
All rights reserved.

Sterling ISBN 0-8069-0848-3

DEDICATION

Thanks to all the sewing machine companies and educators that have supported me throughout the years. Thank you to JoAnn Pugh-Gannon for the opportunity to do this book. And special thanks to my husband Bill for his confidence, support and belief that "I can do it."

The sewing machine's basic stitch formation has not changed since Elias Howe, Jr. patented the first machine in 1846. What has changed though, is the machine's capabilities with an ever-increasing variety of features that speed sewing and allow the homesewer the ability to use a variety of fabrics and a wide range of techniques for professional results.

Machines have come a long way in 150 or so years. Perhaps, like me you learned to sew on a machine that went forward and backward in a straight stitch only. It wasn't "user friendly" and seemed to jam threads constantly and the bobbin was always up to something funky.

Today's machines offer a multitude of features in addition to forward and backward. You can purchase a machine with an infinite number of stitch combinations, computer interfacing capabilities, scanning devices, multi-color stitching options, alphabet choices, multi-language readouts and lighted displays giving you the information needed to complete a task. It may seem overwhelming at times if you haven't shopped lately.

Whether you are purchasing a machine for the first time or looking to upgrade your sewing machine this book is for you. Shopping tips and a buyer's checklist are included to help you make an informed purchase. After all, buying a sewing machine will involve a considerable outlay of cash, so take your time reviewing this information and choose the machine that's right for you.

This book is designed for every beginner, novice or advanced sewer who wants to learn how to make the most of your sewing machine. My intention is

to help you sew better by understanding the fundamentals of sewing machine operation and to learn how to choose needles, thread, presser feet suitable for the fabric and technique. You'll never fear a sewing project again! Ease your tension worries with basic how-to steps for adjusting tension for most sewing operations.

Or just maybe, you are having problems with your sewing machine. Every sewer, experienced or not, has times when everything seems to go wrong—threads break, stitches skip, seams pucker. Refer to the simple troubleshooting guide in the Appendix and learn how to diagnose common sewing problems and perform simple cleaning and maintenance tasks to keep your machine up and running like a charm. Tips are given throughout the book to further assist you with time-saving techniques, new ideas and handy information for your sewing.

My goal is to help you get the most from your sewing machine and to enjoy sewing as much as I do. Happy stitching!

Karen Kunkel
Albany, New York

SHOPPING DECISIONS

Shopping for a new machine or looking to upgrade your present model? Here are some pointers to help you make your decision more easily.

What To Look For When Shopping For A Machine

The first step when choosing a sewing machine is to decide which type of machine suits your particular needs, your sewing skills, and fits your budget. Don't get swayed by a fast talking salesperson and showy demonstration. All the bells and whistles are great, but if you sew occasionally are they really necessary? A good well-made machine will last a lifetime if properly cared for and serviced. Consider a reconditioned machine to get more features for the money.

A wise consumer will shop around and consider several dealers and brands of machines before making a final decision. Purchasing a sewing machine is an individual decision and there is no best model/brand for everyone. The best machine for you is one that you feel the most comfortable with.

At first it may seem like an overwhelming task to choose just one machine. Before you buy, become familiar with machine types, features, and add-ons.

Basic types of machines consist of mechanical or non-computer, electronic, and computerized models. Although all-mechanical machines are still available, electronics have been added to most machine models to make them easier to operate and increase their speed and needle penetration. Electronics merely means electrical signals replace some mechanical switches, levers, and gears.

Noncomputer

These basic machines have manual adjustments and are less complex than computerized models. Most have electronic speed controllers for full needle penetration power for sewing various fabric weights even at the slowest speed. Mechanical foot controllers will tend to lose power as the machine loses speed, so it becomes more difficult to stitch through heavy weight and multiple layers of fabric. In general, electronic foot controllers are more reliable.

Another mechanical feature may include an electronic control. An electric current is transmitted with the touch of a button to select a stitch or move the needle up or down. Without this feature, all operations are done manually.

Non-computer machines can be:

1. Basic zigzag machine
2. Semi-automatic — Have basic zigzag-type stitches as well as variable needle positions, decorative stitches including satin-stitch patterns.
3. Automatic — Will have the same features as a semi-automatic with the addition of a built-in buttonholer which automatically stitches the correct size.

Computerized

Computer machines are controlled by a built-in micro-processor. They have a full range of features including a one-step built-in buttonholer often in various styles, such as keyhole, rounded and knit buttonholes, pre-programmed motifs, and alphabets with features to alter the designs.

Computer machines have memory which is responsible for the expansion of the machine's creative capabilities. As you select a zigzag stitch, for example, the machine automatically adjusts for the ideal settings, which are in the memory.

With memory it is possible to combine or program a string of stitches in a certain sequence into memory, or write with the machine's built-in alphabet and numbers. The latest technology allows the user to interface with a personal computer for customizing designs and converting them into stitching on the machine.

Portable vs. Built-in

All machines are portable and can be placed on any table for sewing. Many have built-in carrying handles and are lighter weight models specifically marketed for toting to sewing classes. Most all machines, whether flatbed or freearm, can be mounted into a cabinet specially designed for sewing. These cabinets give you a convenient work space and storage in one piece of furniture.

TIP: If you already have a sewing machine cabinet that you want a new machine to fit into, make sure the freearm machine has accommodations for a flatbed cabinet.

A Buyers Guide: Getting the best value

Where to Shop?

Independent dealer, discount and department stores, and home shopping clubs are your options.

Before you buy, assess the salesperson's knowledge. What is the store's reputation? Will the dealer stand behind the machine if you are not satisfied? Prices might seem enticing at some discount and mail-order services, but service and information may be the trade-off.

Your safest bet is to purchase a machine from a reputable dealer who offers a thorough demonstration and good after-sale service. The machine may cost slightly more but a local dealer may be worth the additional expense for guaranteed continued satisfaction. Many offer additional instruction for high-end models. Ask about videos and other support materials. A dealer who is concerned about you learning how to use your new machine will make the experience beneficial for both of you.

TIP: For sewers on the go, consider purchasing a padded sewing machine bag with a shoulder strap— a practical accessory for people who take their sewing machine everywhere.

TIP: You might want to avoid those one-day hotel sales since they tend to be gimmicky. Remember, one-day the sales-people will not be there after the sale.

What's Your Budget?

Does the store take trade-ins towards the purchase of a new machine? What's your used sewing machine worth? Check the current issue of the Sewing Machine Blue Book which is updated annually to provide current retail value estimates. Many sewing machine dealers have a Blue Book for you to review.

Features to Look For:

Even the most basic features, such as threading and bob-bin winding, should not be overlooked. Other features to consider include:

- Color-coded stitch selection—a variety of stitches built-in for various tasks?
- A wide range of accessories or attachments—buttonhole foot, zipper foot, blindhem foot or snap-on presser feet?
- Freearm capability for stitching around small areas — pant legs, sleeves or cuffs.
- Automatic tension—numbered dial?
- Pressure adjustment for presser feet—necessary for all fabrics?
- Stitch length and width selection—easy to adjust?
- Are variable speeds included—or is the sewing speed easy to control?
- A built-in buttonhole mechanism—one-step or more?

Now move on to the machine's special features. How are the stitches selected? Are the dials easy to read and turn? How is the buttonhole stitched?

The Test Drive

Test drive as many machines as you can using scraps of your own fabric, not the stiff demo cloth provided at some of the stores. Consider bringing a selection of different fabric weights and types—ones that you most often sew with and the ones you have been avoiding including thin silkies, slippery synthetics, heavy denim, and knits that stretch. How does the machine handle them? How did the fabric feed under the presser foot? A good quality machine will sew straight and evenly without pulling or veering off to one side. Do the feed dogs hold lighter weight fabric firmly? Check the machines stitches to be sure they are even and the fabric is without puckers. Did it "creep" or get "sucked into" the needle plate? Is the tension balanced, are there any skipped stitches, or does the machine jam? How does the machine handle bulky fabrics and multiple layers?

Try out the threading and bobbin-winding procedures for ease of use. Check out the instructional manual for readability. Is it clearly written and easy to follow?

You may also want to try out some of the accessories that come with the machine. Are they easy to use? Will they be useful with your type of sewing?

Allow yourself plenty of time for testing and evaluating the machine. Try to shop at off-peak times—a time when you won't be rushed or hurried. If you don't have the opportunity to test everything in one day, plan a second trip to the shop. Take your stitch samples home and evaluate them. Thorough study and evaluation will help you make a careful, well-informed decision.

Perform the same test on all models you are considering for a fair comparison. Don't compare a top-of-the-line computer model, however, with a no-frills mechanical machine and expect them to perform equally.

Do you plan to use the machine as a portable model, if so, is there a built-in handle? How much does the machine actually weigh? Is it truly portable?

Is the machine easy to care for and maintain? Are the coverplates easy to access and remove for darning or cleaning? Can you replace the lightbulb easily?

Warranties

Are there any limitations? In general, parts are included but labor is not. Check to see if the store offers free labor for a period of time.

SHOPPING DECISIONS

TIP: It is a good idea to keep a record of your machine's serial number, model number and date of purchase for future reference. Remember to send in your warranty card that comes with the machine.

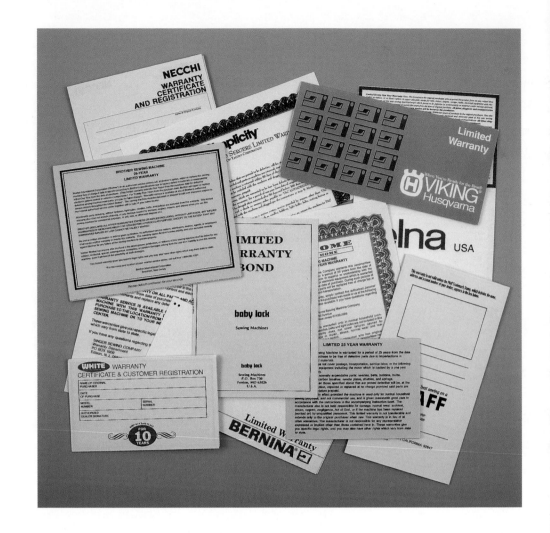

Most sewing machine manufacturers offer a 10- to 25-year guarantee on mechanical parts; 1- to 5-year warranty on electrical components, and 90 days on everything else. Electronic parts may have a separate 2- to 5-year warranty. Your local sewing machine dealer may offer their own warranty or free service for 1 year, although others may not—it doesn't hurt to ask what the dealer's policy is.

Training Classes

What kind of lessons does the dealer offer? Is there a customer service person available by phone to help with sewing problems? Will you be kept up-to-date on new accessories? Is a newsletter available? What about a sewing club in the store where you can learn new sewing techniques? Can you meet the teacher or sit in on one of the lessons before your decide? Is there an instructional video available?

Service

What is the turnover time for an average repair? Are loaner machines available if yours will be in the shop for a period of time? Is the repair done on-site? Does the store stock parts?

The Purchase

Once you've decided on the perfect machine, be sure it's just that. Before you bring your machine home, unpack it and test it right in the store. Learn how to thread the top, wind a bobbin, and make sure the tension is correct.

Upgrade Policy

If you should decide to upgrade your machine within a certain amount of time, what will you get back for your machine?

Buyer Beware

When a salesperson or an advertisement stresses these features, don't be swayed. Understand and learn what they are talking about.

- "100% jam-proof"—All machines may jam at one time or another.
- "Automatic tension"—Can it be overridden? From time to time you will need to adjust the thread tension yourself.
- "All-metal machine"—Ask to see the internal metal parts.
- "Oscillating or rotary bobbin system"—The oscillating hook catches the needle thread as it swings back and forth in a semi-circle; the rotary hook travels in a cotinuous circle, hooking the needle thread on each rotation. Which system makes a better stitch for your work?
- "Heavy-duty sewing machine designed to sew all fabrics without adjustments"—Test drive with your fabrics.
- "Built-in serger stitch"—Are they just referring to a zigzag stitch?
- "One-day only hotel sales" or "School models ordered but were unsold due to budget cuts"— Often advertised as come on's. Beware!
- "Sale of the century"—Remember there will always be another.
- "Must buy today to get this price"—Don't be rushed, take your time to decide.

Let's Shop

Here are some of the questions you should ask yourself and the sewing machine dealer before purchasing a machine:

1. How much sewing do you plan to do?

2. How much can you afford to spend?

3. What type of fabrics will you be sewing with and how does the machine handle them?

4. How many features does the machine have and will you use them? Remember the more stitches/features the higher the cost.

5. Can the machine be updated with additional stitch patterns on design discs or cards and/or attachments?

6. Does the dealer have a good reputation?

7. Is service done on the premises or will your machine need to be sent out to be repaired?

8. Does the store offer training classes?

Choosing a Sewing Machine for Young Stitchers

Toy companies do have machines on the market that are small, lightweight, battery-operated, plastic machines designed so a child can use them without adult supervision. But if you're looking to introduce a young person to his or her first real sewing machine, there are basic models offered by most sewing machine brands available at your local sewing machine dealership. Of course, these real plug-in models should be operated with care, keeping safety precautions in mind.

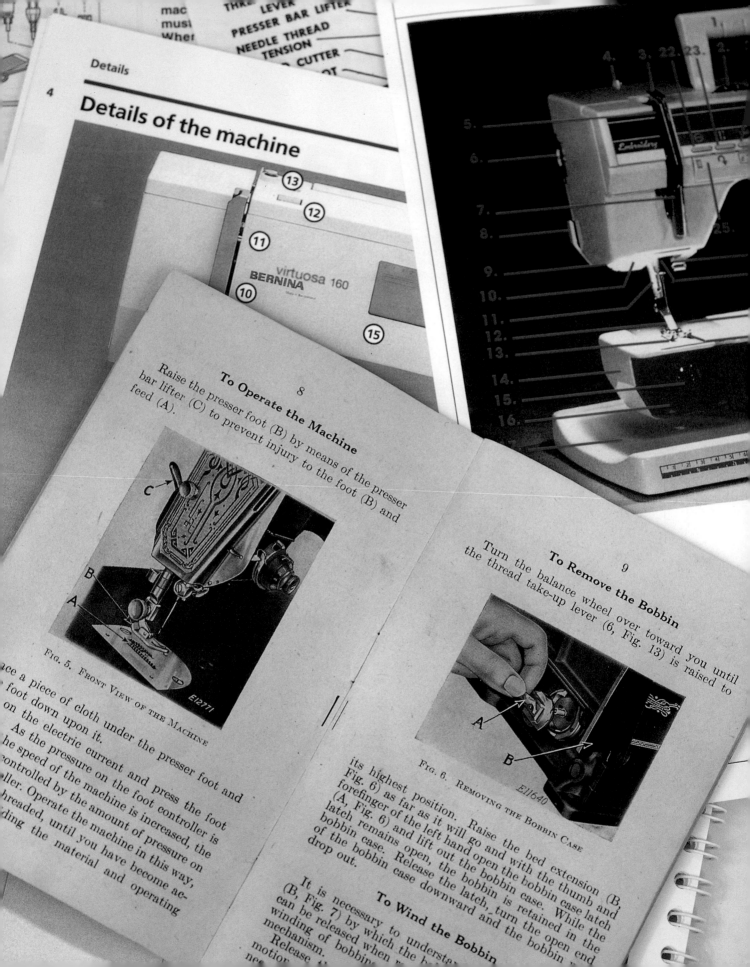

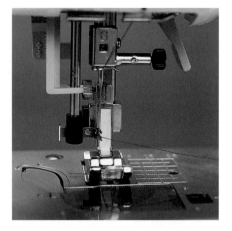

GETTING TO KNOW YOUR MACHINE

With all the different types and brands of sewing machines available, it's good to remember that all are fundamentally similar. The basic operating parts labeled in the photograph are common to most machines. I have found that many of the instruction manuals that come with a machine tend to be sketchy. That is why this chapter is devoted to listing and labeling the parts of your machine and explaining their importance to your sewing.

Principal Parts Of The Sewing Machine

Whether you have a basic mechanical or a sophisticated computer machine the basic parts are common on all models.

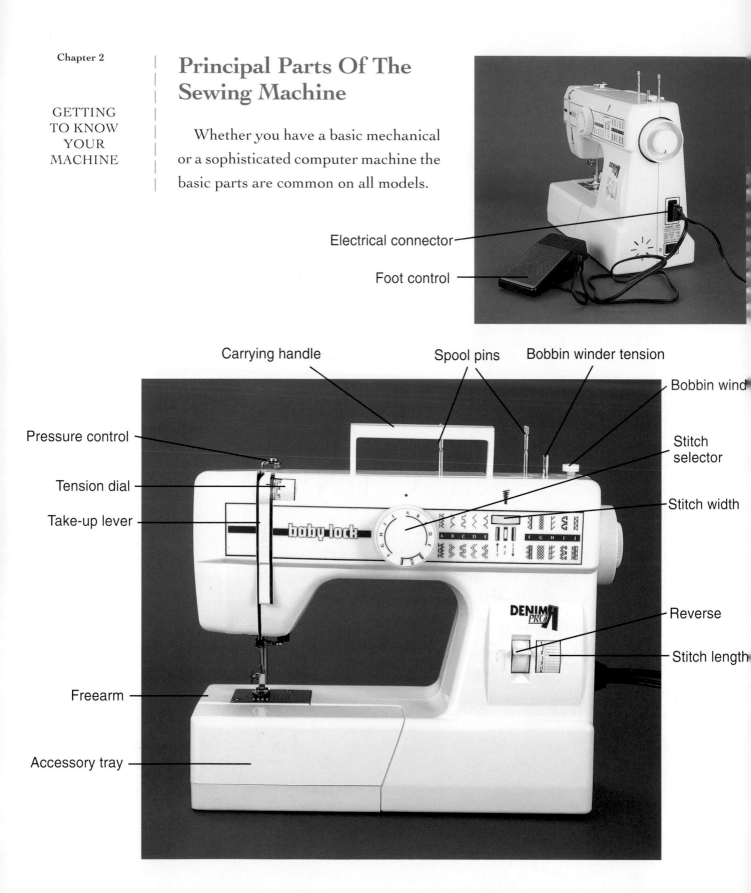

Electrical connector

Foot control

Carrying handle

Spool pins

Bobbin winder tension

Bobbin wind

Pressure control

Tension dial

Take-up lever

Stitch selector

Stitch width

Reverse

Stitch length

Freearm

Accessory tray

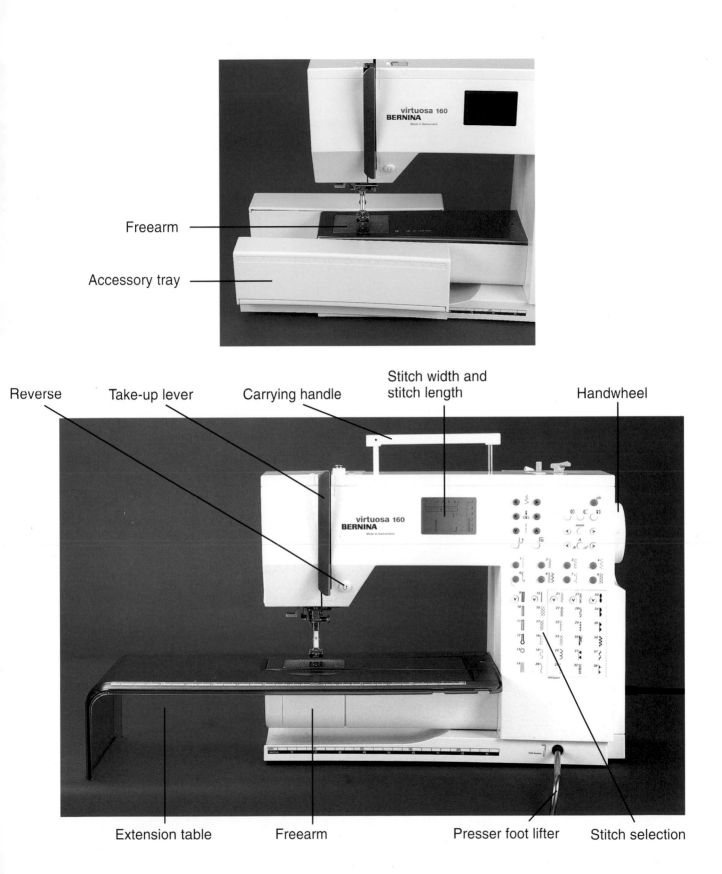

Freearm

Accessory tray

Reverse   Take-up lever   Carrying handle

Stitch width and
stitch length

Handwheel

virtuosa 160
BERNINA
Made in Switzerland

Extension table   Freearm   Presser foot lifter   Stitch selection

25

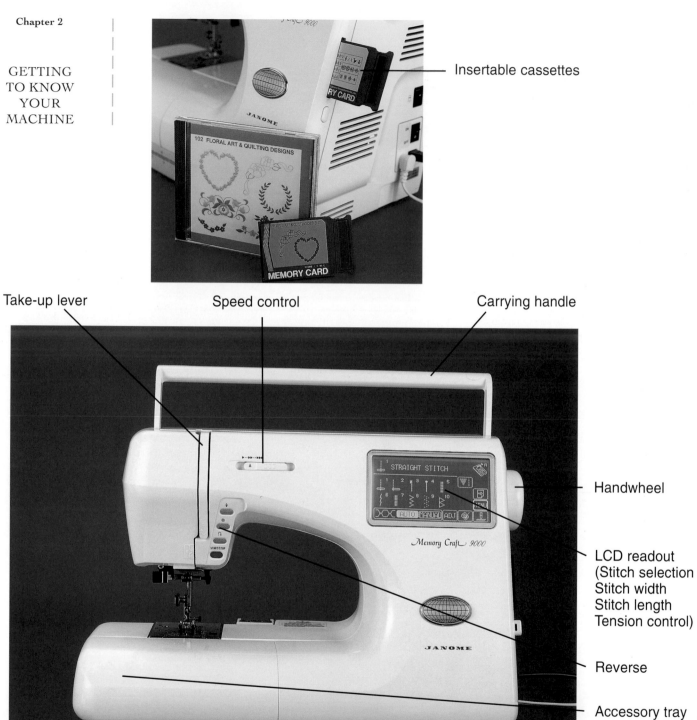

Insertable cassettes

Take-up lever

Speed control

Carrying handle

Handwheel

LCD readout
(Stitch selection
Stitch width
Stitch length
Tension control)

Reverse

Accessory tray

Presser fool lifter

Extension table—Detachable sewing table lifts out or slides off out of the way to convert the machine from a flatbed to a free-arm. Often it will have a storage compartment that opens out on the front for storing sewing accessories.

Free arm—Allows you to stitch small circular areas in garment construction such as cuffs, pant leg hems, arm holes and the like.

Pressure control—Regulates the amount of pressure exerted by the presser foot. Decrease the pressure to sew heavy fabrics and multiple layers smoothly. (Fig. 1, 2, and 3) Increase the pressure for fine or thin fabrics.

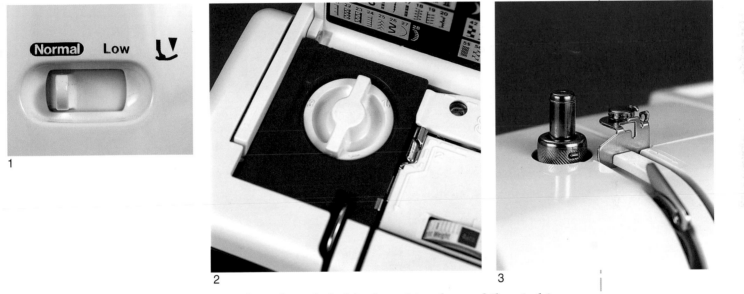

1

2

3

Thread take-up lever—Important thread guide holds thread in place while stitching.

Bobbin winder tension—If the bobbin does not wind evenly or stops before it is full, turn the adjustment screw to the right to tighten, left to loosen.

Spool pin or spool holder—A vertical or horizontal spool pin is provided on top of the machine to hold the thread in place. Most have a spool pin cover, one for small spools and one for larger spools.

Drop feed lever — Lowers the feed dogs for free-motion or free-hand sewing used in quilting, button sewing, embroidery and monogramming. (Fig. 1, 2, and 3)

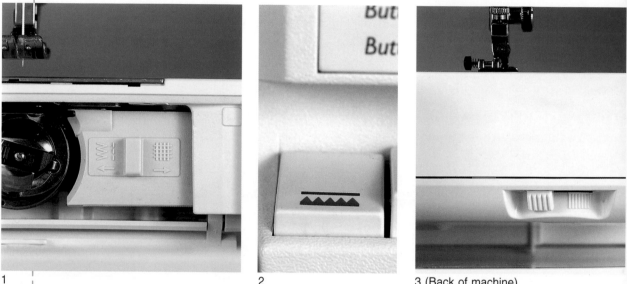

1   2   3 (Back of machine)

Bobbin winder — Winds thread onto a bobbin and will stop automatically when full. A thread cutter may be located under the bobbin winder or off to the side. An automatic clutch is now available on most machines to automatically disengage the needle when the bobbin winder is pushed to the right to wind a bobbin.

Push-pull clutch — Automatic clutch disengages the needle from regular sewing for bobbin winding. Pull out to release for bobbin winding and push to engage needle again.

Stitch length selector — For regulating stitch length from 0 up to 6mm. Many are color-coded to easily locate various stitches.

Stitch width selector — Makes the width of the stitches narrow or wide.

Needle position selector — Places the needle in any of three positions; left, right or middle. Computer models can have infinite needle positions.

Stitch selector — Choose from a number of built-in stitches with a turn of a dial, lever, or push a button.

Tension dial (selector) — Regulates the upper thread tension. (Fig. 1 and 2)

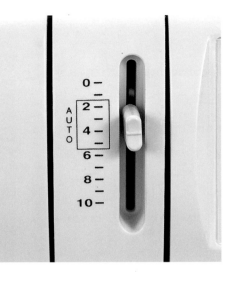

Reverse — Sew in reverse to lock and tie off stitches instantly with a touch of a button or lift of a lever. Most will feed the fabric backwards only while the lever is pressed.

1

2

Power switch — Turns the machine off and on.

Sewing Light — A built-in light directly above the needle and sewing area illuminates working surface. The light bulb can be changed by removing the face cover. Consult your owners manual for exact information.

Carrying handle — Makes the machine easy to carry and portable. Most handles are retractable.

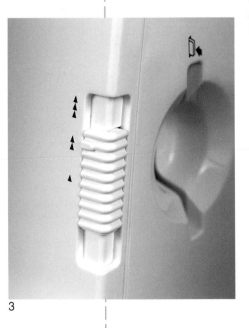

Handwheel — Located on the right side of the machine.

Electrical Connector and Foot Control — With the foot control you can start and stop sewing and regulate speed. This allows your hands to be free for sewing.

Speed control — Stitching speed usually has two ranges slow and fast, some can moderate in between. (Fig. 3 and 4)

3

Presser foot lifter — An L-shape extension lever, operated by the knee, that raises and lowers the presser foot enabling you to keep both hands on the fabric.

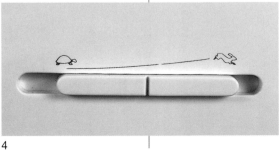

4

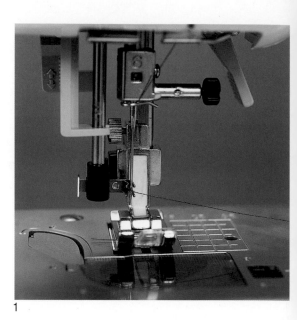

1

Computerized model machines will also have these parts:

Integrated needle threader—Built-in threader helps to thread the machine's needle. (Fig. 1)

LCD (liquid crystal display) readout—A display window on some computerized machines provides sewing information with a message button to indicate recommended presser foot, stitch width and length, and pressure adjustment for each stitch. (Fig. 2)

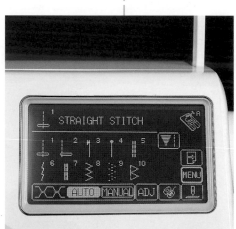

2

Automatic one-step buttonholer in various styles—Square, round, keyhole, stretch.

Touch-pad stitch selection—One-touch selects a stitch. (Fig. 2)

Memory function—Programs a combination of designs into the machine's memory.

Built-in letters and numbers—Available in various styles and/or sizes.

Mirror image function—Flips a design motif to be stitched out in its mirror image.

Automatic thread cutter button—Cuts upper and lower threads automatically and places the needle in its highest position. (Fig. 3)

Needle up/down button—Places the needle either in the up or down position when stitch is completed.

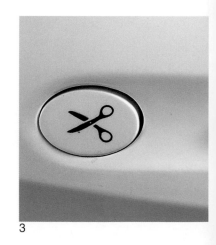

3

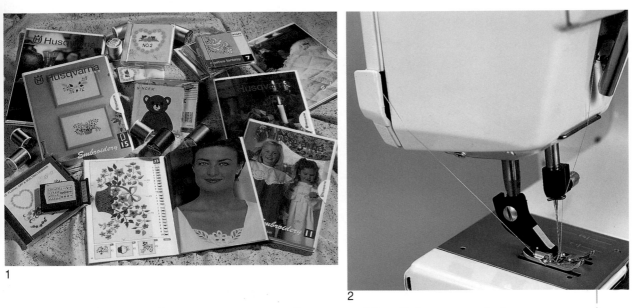

1

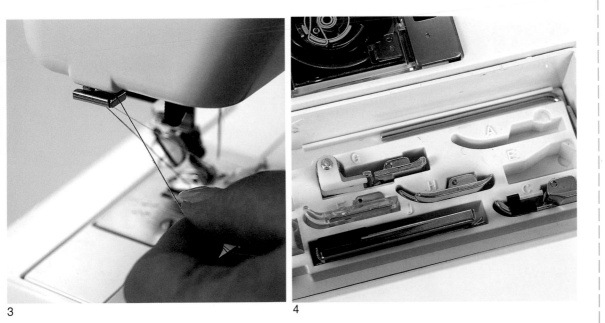

2

Memory cards, cartridges or cassettes—Computer "discs" that sort stitches or patterns, enabling you to expand the machine's capabilities. (Fig. 1)

Thread cutter—Is provided on the bottom of the face cover or behind the needle bar for quick thread cutting. (Fig. 2 and 3)

Needle bar—Moves needle up and down

All-purpose presser foot—Many are snap-on for ease. (Fig. 4)

3

4

Thread cutter

Needle clamp

Thread guide

Needle

Presser foot

Needle plate

Feed dogs

Bobbin case

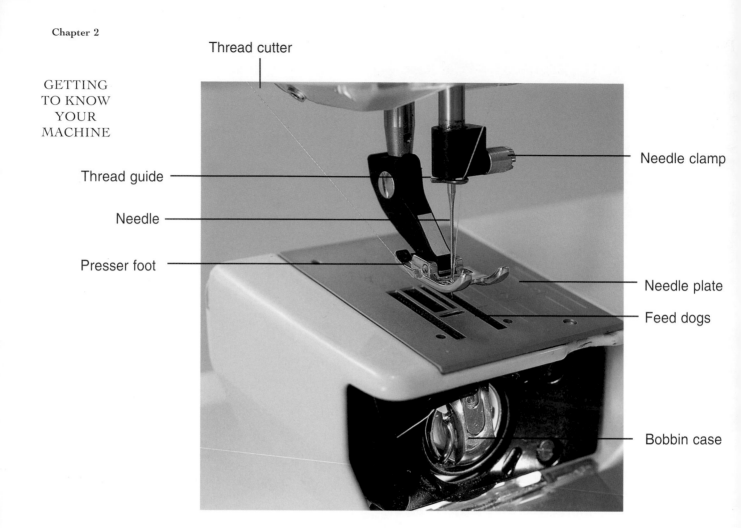

Thread guide — Holds thread in place above needle

Needle clamp — Holds needle in position for sewing

Feed dogs — The "teeth" under the presser foot moves the fabric into position for stitching. On most machines, the feed dogs can be lowered to eliminate the feed for free-motion work.

Needle plate — Usually has an etched guide for accurate stitching.

Bobbin case — Holds lower thread(bobbin) in place

Slide plate — Covers the bobbin area. Slides off or opens to display the bobbin.

Basic Machine Accessories

Most sewing machines companies provide you with a minimal supply of accessories to get started.

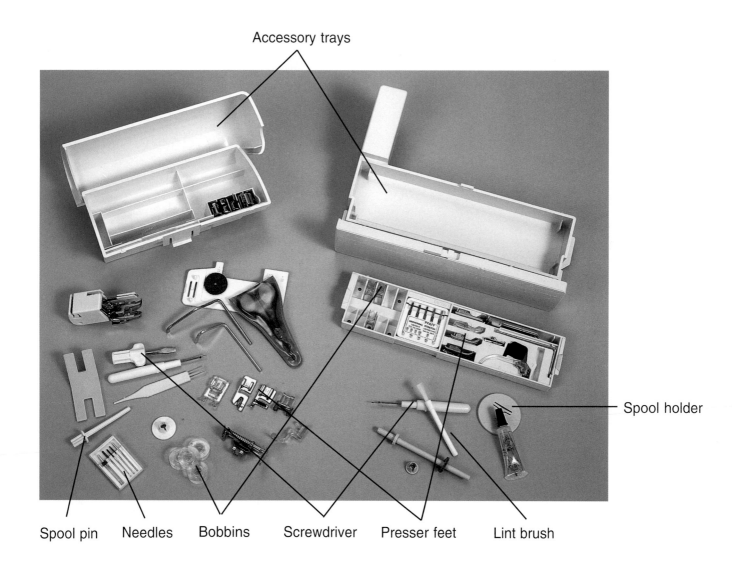

Accessory trays

Spool holder

Spool pin   Needles   Bobbins   Screwdriver   Presser feet   Lint brush

Accessory pouch or tray

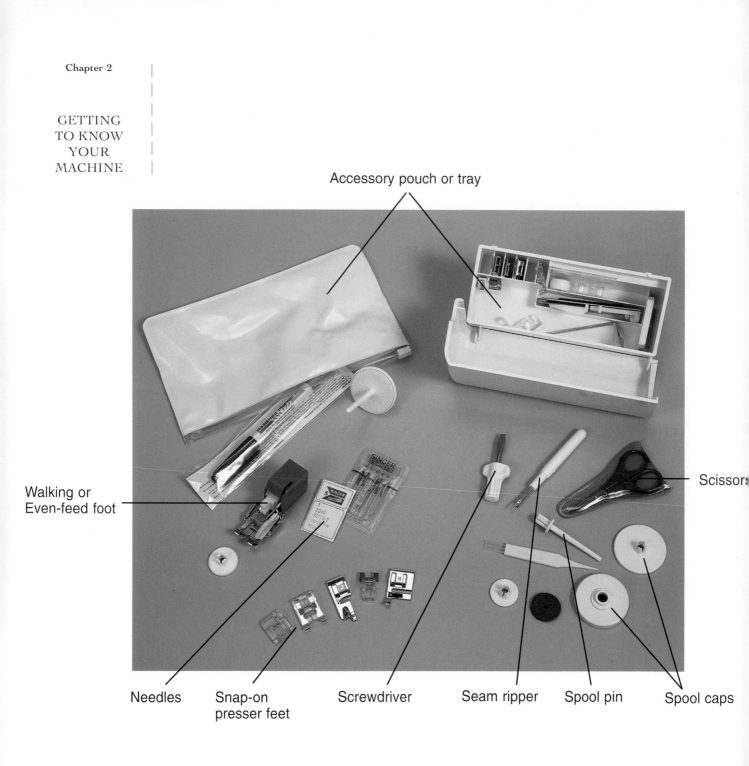

Walking or
Even-feed foot

Scissors

Needles

Snap-on
presser feet

Screwdriver

Seam ripper

Spool pin

Spool caps

What A Notion!

In addition to your sewing machine, you will also need some special tools and equipment before getting started.

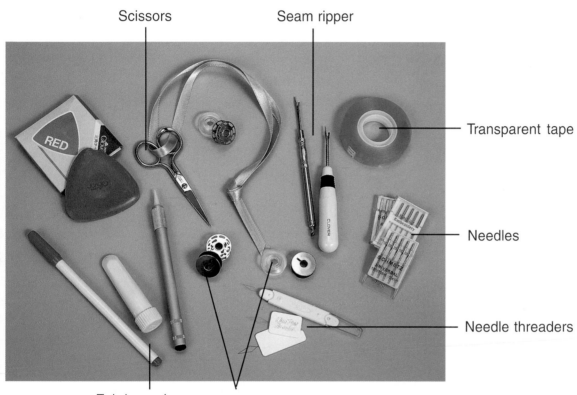

Scissors Seam ripper

Transparent tape

Needles

Needle threaders

Fabric markers Bobbins

Scissors for trimming threads. I like to tie a ribbon through the thumb and finger hole of the scissors and hang them around my neck so my scissors are always handy.

Seam ripper (if the machine does not come with one) for removing threads. No matter how good a sewer you are, there's always a need for a seam ripper.

Extra needles are a necessity. You can never have too many.

Extra bobbins to save time. Always have your basic colors wound on extra bobbins.

Fabric markers are essential to any sewer. Air- and water-soluble fabric markers are handy for marking placement for buttonholes and transferring placement lines for decorative stitching.

Transparent tape or Scotch brand Magic Tape™ can be stitched through without gumming up the needle. Use it to position buttons, zippers, appliqués, and various other tasks.

Liquid seam sealant prevents fabric from raveling excessively. It works to tie off threads and to clean up buttonholes. Fray-Check® is one brand of seam sealant.

A needle threader often comes with the machine or is built-in. If your machine doesn't have one, purchase a separate threader. It works by pulling thread across the notched head of the threader, then glides the thread down to the needles eye. Gently press, and the head pushes the thread into the eye. They are helpful for threading your machine when working with heavier threads.

A spring hoop is useful for darning, and free-hand embroidery, and appliqué. They are easy to use because they are narrow enough to fit under the presser foot of the machine. (Fig. 1)

Tear-away or wash-away stabilizers will be particularly helpful when doing machine embroidery to minimize puckering. (Fig 1)

Interfacings iron-on or sew in to stabilize your fabric to prevent stretching. They often come in handy when doing machine embroidery when large areas need stabilization. (Fig. 1)

1

Specialty Notions

A **Pedal-Stay**® is a machine pedal holder with are non-skid bottom which keeps your sewing machine pedal from creeping away from you. Instead of a purchasing a Pedal-Stay, consider using a non-slip mat that grips the floor to place beneath your machine pedal. (Fig. 1 and 2) Another option is hot glue. Simply use your glue gun and apply a fair amount of glue to the underside of the pedal. Allow to dry. The dried glue creates a non-skid surface on the bottom of the pedal.

A **magnetic pincushion** is a handy pin catcher. Another type of magnetic pin cushion has a peal away adhesive on the back can be stuck to the bed of to your sewing machine to be used as is a handy pin catcher. (Fig. 3)

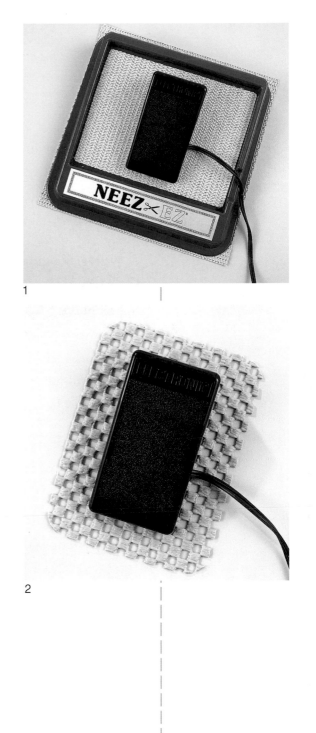

1

2

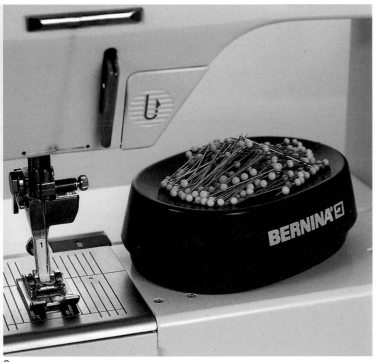

3

A **magnifier** attaches to the table or the front of the machine and is designed for close work. On the table mounted version, a swing arm allows you to move the magnifier in front of the machine when needed. Often a light is attached. (Fig. 1)

Perfect Posture is for sewers who spend lots of time leaning into a sewing machine. Give your back a break while sitting at your sewing machine with **Body Rite® Posture Pleasure**. A specially designed wearable weight prevents your shoulders from rolling forward and helps maintain a proper posture. It reduces neck, shoulder and back pain.

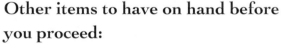

1

Other items to have on hand before you proceed:

- Your sewing machine owner's manual
- Scrap fabrics for test sewing
- Notebook to record your machine's settings and a place for your practice scraps. I like to use a loose leaf binder and plastic page protectors. It makes an ideal reference book. Some companies offer owner's handbooks written especially for a particular model which helps take you beyond the basics, from practical to decorative stitches and techniques with model specific explanations. (Fig. 2)

2

Your Sewing Area

Before you begin, set up a sewing area for stress-free stitching. Whether or not you have a separate room designated for sewing, here are some ideas to make your space efficient and pleasant.

A little-used office, guest room, attic or basement make great candidates for a sewing room, but if none of these are available, take a tour of your home for a space that can be used for a sewing machine set-up. A storage closet, for example, can be large enough to place a table or desk against the back wall to hold your machine. Consider electrical outlet availability and lighting. Install shelves in the upper section of the closet for notions and fabric storage. A common family space can possibly be reconfigured to fit a sewing area. Use book cases or screens to separate your sewing from the rest of the room.

After finding your space, choose a sturdy sewing table or desk that is vibration-free. The most desirable working surface should be approximately 26" to 38" from the floor so the machine bed is at a 30" height for an average person of 5' 5". Sewing tables are available from sewing machine stores and through sewing notions and equipment mail-order catalogs. Some stores may offer custom-built furniture.

Invest in a comfortable chair. It will help increase your sewing stamina. I like a secretary's chair that swivels and rolls. It has an adjustable back and seat and a built-in lumbar support. When you're sewing, adjust the chair height so your forearms are parallel to the floor. Keep your head and neck upright and your feet flat on the floor. Support your back by adjusting the chair or use a back rest to support your lower back.

Good lighting is important to your sewing comfort. In addition to natural lighting (if available) and a ceiling light, consider adding lighting over your work space. A desk lamp with an adjustable arm works well. Position the lamp over your work to eliminate shadows. Track lights are geared to shine down in front and behind your work, and most are adjustable.

TIP: Lost or misplaced your sewing machine owner's manual? Contact your local dealer, or write to the manufacturer for a new one. Include your model number which should be stamped on the machine either on the back or on the front of a flatbed model.

NEEDLES AND THREAD

Needles and thread are often overlooked when it comes to machine stitching. These basic notions should be considered together since they are vital to your stitching success. As you review this chapter, you will learn there is no one thread or needle to satisfy all sewing needs. Both are selected according to the fabric type, weight and the stitching technique whether you are sewing construction details or adding decorative touches. Handy reference charts are provided as invaluable guides for needle and thread selection.

How the Sewing Machine Works

Two of the most integral parts of the sewing machine are the needle and thread. They work together to form the stitch. The upper thread, carried by the needle, interlocks with the lower thread, carried by the shuttle hook, forming a locked stitch just like the first machine ever invented.

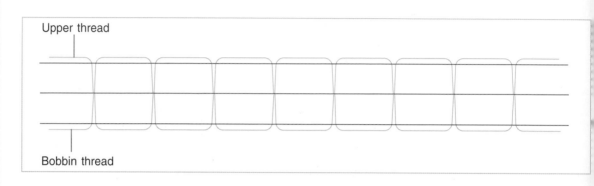

The needle delivers thread from the machine's inner workings to where the stitch forms. The correct needle is often the key to successful stitching. Sewing machine manufacturers will suggest changing the machine's needle after 8 hours of stitching or after every project. It is also important to select the correct needle size to match your fabric.

In general, the finer the fabric the smaller the needle size should be. Sewing machine needles are identified with 2 numbers 75/11 or 80/12. The higher number indicates the metric size and the lower refers to the US imperial system. Needles range in size from fine 60/8 to heavy-duty 120/19. For general sewing, sizes 11 and 14 are most commonly used. The correct-size needle should be small enough to pierce the fabric without leaving a hole, but have a large enough eye for the thread. Use the chart provided here to help you select the correct size appropriate for your fabric.

Using the proper needle size is as important as the correct type. This table suggests needle type and size for various fabrics.

FABRIC	NEEDLE TYPE AND SIZE
Woven types such as linen, chiffon, batiste, organdy, wool, and velvet	Universal sharp-point needle, sized 11–14(80–90)
Knitted types, cotton, wool, and synthetics	Fine ballpoint needle, sized 11–14(80–90)
Dense knits	Medium ballpoint needle, sized 11–14(80–90)
Stretch fabrics	Medium ballpoint or stretch needle, sized 11–14(80–90)
Densely woven such as twill, denim, duck, and canvas	Denim needle, sized 11–14(80–90)
Leather, suede, imitation leather and suedes, vinyl, and plastics	Leather needle, sized 12–16(80–90)

General-purpose needles include universal, sharp-point, and ballpoint. Specialty needles are denim, stretch, topstitch, leather, hemstitch, quilting, machine embroidery, metallic, and self-threading. Double needles and triple needles are also available in denim, stretch, machine embroidery, hemstitch, and extra-wide widths.

The Needle

The needle penetrates the fabric and carries the thread through the material. Parts of the needle are the shank, shaft, long groove, eye, scarf, point, and short groove. Each part is designed for a specific purpose.

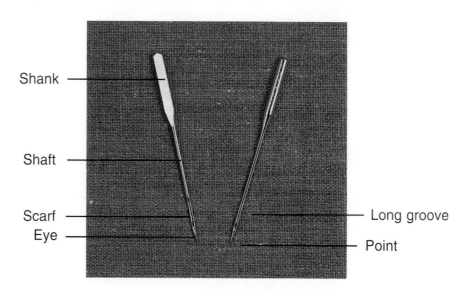

Shank

Shaft

Scarf

Eye

Long groove

Point

The **shank** or upper part of the needle has one flat side that fits into the needle bar and is held in by the needle clamp. One side of the shank is flat, and the other rounded.

The **shaft** or lower part of the needle extends from the shank to the needle's point. The shaft size is determined by the needle size; the smaller the needle size the thinner the shaft.

The **long groove** is on the same side as the rounded part of the shank. The groove guides the thread into the needle eye.

The **eye** of the needle is just above the point. It is proportioned to the size of the needle.

The **scarf** is an indentation behind the eye which allows the needle thread to form a loop and make a stitch.

The **point** of the needle penetrates the fabric.

NEEDLE KNOW HOW

General Purpose Needles

Universal needle	Universal point is slightly rounded and sharp. It is best for general-purpose sewing on most knit and woven fabrics.
Sharp needle	With its very sharp point and slender shaft, it is best used for topstitching and edgestitching on fine woven fabrics such as silk and microfibers.
Ballpoint needle	The slightly rounded point spreads knitted fibers apart rather than piercing them for smooth stitching on knitted fabrics. Use for interlock knit fabric, mesh and coarse knits that tend to run if snagged.

Specialty Needles

Denim needle	For densely woven fabrics like denim, duck, and canvas, this needle has a slender point and strong shaft.
Stretch needle	Has a slightly rounded point for stitching elasticized fabrics in activewear sewing.
Topstitch needle	Designed with an extra-large eye and deeper grove for use with thicker weight decorative threads or double strands for more pronounced stitching.
Leather needle	Shaped like a wedge, the point pierces the fabric to make a hole to stitch leather and heavy non-woven synthetics.
Quilting needle	The shaft tapers to the point to prevent damage to delicate heirloom quilting fabrics and for stitching mulitible layers.
Metallic needle	For stitching weaker metallic threads that shred and split. The eye of the needle is larger to accomodate heavier thread weights.
Embroidery needle	Has a larger and special scarf for stitching with specialty threads such as rayon, silk, and acrylic.
Self-threading needle	For general purpose, this needle has a special slip-in slot for threading. Designed for sewers who have difficulty threading a needle.

NEEDLES AND THREADS

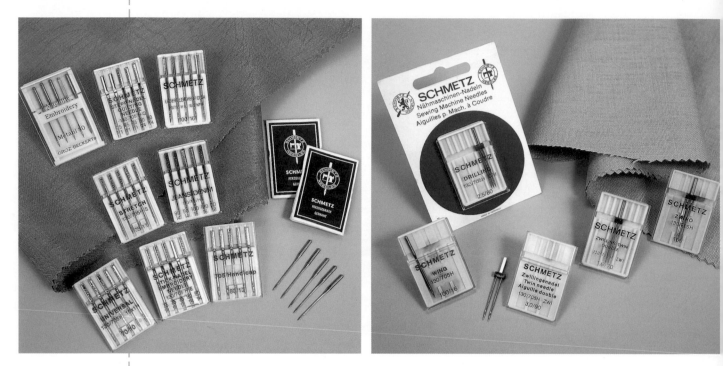

Special Purpose Needles

Double needle*	Constructed with 2 needles on a crossbar from a single shaft. Use for techniques such as topstitching, pintucks, hemming knit garments, and decorative stitch patterns.
Triple needle*	Constructed with 3 needles on a crossbar from a single shaft. Use for techniques such as topstitching, pintucks, hemming knit garments, and decorative stitch patterns.
Spring needle*	Designed for free-motion embroidery, these needles have a wire spring above the point to prevent the fabric from pulling up when being stitched without the feed dogs.

*Double and triple needles are available in denim, stretch, and embroidery versions.

Inserting a Needle

   Proper needle insertion is important to the operation of your sewing machine. After choosing the proper needle, refer to your machine owner's manual for specifics.

   To insert a needle, loosen the needle clamp screw with the small screwdriver that comes with your machine (in the accessory package). Then, with the flat side of the shank facing away from you, push the needle up into the clamp as far as it will go. Tighten the clamp using the small screwdriver. In general, to remove a needle, reverse the insertion process.

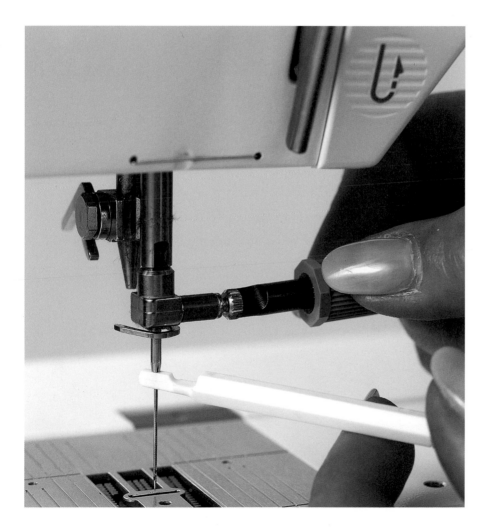

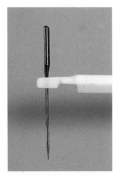

TIP: Here's a sharp idea: a needle inserter. The inserter holds the needle in a tapered hole while you tighten the needle clamp screw. This is helpful for people with arthritic hands.

Getting to the Point

Many stitching problems can be attributed to the needle. Here are just a few:

Improper insertion — No stitches being formed or skipped stitches may be due to incorrect needle insertion. Be sure the needle is all the way up into the needle clamp and the flat side is to the back (this may vary on some machines — check your manual).

Incorrect size — Stitches may look unbalanced if the wrong-size needle is used for the machine and fabric. A too-fine needle will fray the fabric and a too-heavy needle will poke large holes in a fine fabric. See the table on page 43 for correct needle size.

Bent, burred, or dull needle — A damaged needle will undoubtedly cause stitching problems. A bent needle causes the fabric to draw to one side, feeding in a curve rather than a straight line. A blunt needle can cause pulls in the fabric. It is a good idea to change your machine needle before you begin a new project.

Needle Check

Place a needle on a flat surface on its flat side and hold it down with your finger. Examine the needle to see if the space along the shaft is parallel to the table. If it is not, it is probably bent; discard it and use a new needle.

All About Thread

As a general rule, fine thread equals fine stitching. Don't be tempted by bargain brand thread. These inexpensive threads are often the cause for many stitching problems—breaking, knotting, skipped stitches, puckered seams just to mention a few. Be kind to your machine by choosing a thread with a smooth even appearance without nubs, uneven thickness, or fuzziness. Look at the thread carefully to judge its quality before purchasing.

TIP: If thread color is being rubbed off on your machine, your thread is inferior and should not be used.

Poor-quality thread will have a fuzzy or "hairy" appearance. It will be twisted unevenly with thick and thin areas. High-quality thread is smooth and twisted evenly.

All-purpose thread is the most common and is usually made of cotton-wrapped polyester. It will work for most stitching on light- to medium-weight fabrics. For heavier fabrics, use a long-staple polyester thread with extra strength. Polyester thread is recommended for knit and swimwear fabrics.

49

NEEDLES
AND
THREADS

For decorative stitching, buttonholes, and machine embroidery, specialty threads now are widely available for use on the sewing machine. Specialty threads intensify decorative stitching with their heavier weights, luster, and brilliant colors. Topstitching and buttonhole-twist threads are the most common. Don't be shy about using some of the newer threads available, such as cotton machine-embroidery thread, acrylic, rayon, silk, metallic, and more.

Thread Types

Cotton-wrapped Polyester — This all-purpose thread is ideal for most fabrics and machine stitching. The polyester core gives it strength and elasticity. The cotton outside blends with natural fibers and can withstand higher iron temperatures.

Extra-fine Cotton wrapped Polyester — Designed for light- to medium-weight fabrics for garment construction, this fine thread gives a neat, non-bulky finish with an almost invisible seam.

Cotton — Not as strong as cotton-wrapped polyester, cotton thread is not desirable for seaming. Use 100% cotton thread for decorative stitching because of its subtle luster. Since it has little stretch, it works well for machine embroidery. Cotton thread is available in different weights.

Rayon — Lustrous rayon is not strong, therefore it is not suitable for seaming. Use it when a high-gloss shine is called for. Some brands are static-free to make work easy on any machine. Quality brands won't shrink or fade, and will keep their original shine and luster after washing. Available in a variety of weights from fine to heavy.

TIP: Even though it is convenient, it is not a good idea to use clear nylon monofilament thread in your machine as an all-purpose thread. Sewing machine manufacturers do not recommend this practice because constant use of nylon thread will wear down the thread paths of the sewing machine as well as create friction on the moving parts. It is best to use monofilament thread for decorative purposes only and in the bobbin.

Silk—Silk thread is strong but tends to be costly so it is not often used for garment construction. Silk thread has a high luster and is available in various weights. It is best used for hand-basting, decorative machine embroidery, and distinctive topstitching.

Metallic—This super shiny thread is available in a wide range of solid and variegated colors and is used exclusively for decorative stitching. Today's versions are less wiry than their predecessors and less likely to fray, shred, and break. Metallic thread is available in different weights.

Topstitching—Topstitching or buttonhole-twist thread is widely available for machine stitching. This strong thread is used for decorative sewing rather than for buttonhole stitching. It is too thick for machine-made buttonholes.

TIP: Many decorative threads are available on cones. Cone thread obviously doesn't fit on your sewing machine's spool pin, but thread cone-holders are available. They hold cone thread in place behind your sewing machine and have an extension that guides the thread up to your machine's spool pin and thread guides.

Ribbon-embroidery Thread—Fine, lightweight ribbon is soft and pliable enough for machine sewing. Available on spools or by the yard in narrow 1/16" widths, ribbon floss is used in the bobbin for reverse decorative stitching. Available in silk and polyester.

Nylon Monofilament—Invisible monofilament thread is 100% nylon and resembles a very fine fishing line. Nylon thread is often used in the bobbin for decorative purposes so that it is not necessary to rethread the bobbin with every color change. Beware of some monofilament threads since they tend to be wiry and stiff and will cause stitching difficulties.

Thread Weight

Thread does come in a variety of sizes and weights. A #50-weight thread is for all-purpose stitching. A #30-weight is a heavier machine embroidery thread. A fine, 2-ply thread is a #60-weight. So, the lower the number, the thicker the thread. Or, the higher the number, the finer the thread.

Here's a simple rule to follow when selecting thread: Match sewing thread to the fabric type and weight. In other words, use natural fiber thread for natural fabrics and synthetic thread for synthetic fabrics. A too-heavy thread will not set into the fabric and will remain on the surface—thus causing a weaker stitch.

Another rule of thumb is to select a thread color two shades darker than the fabric. The thread wrapped on the spool will appear darker than when stitched out. So, it is a good idea to unwrap a strand and compare it to your fabric.

How To Thread A Sewing Machine

Threading consists of four operations:

1. Winding the bobbin
2. Threading the bobbin case
3. Threading the upper thread and needle
4. Raising the bobbin thread

Lower Threading

When threading a new machine, follow the threading diagram given in the owner's manual. The lower thread is supplied by a bobbin. The bobbin, located under the needle plate is actually a tiny spool of thread that fits precisely into a bobbin case. Some bobbin cases are built into the machine (Fig. 1) although others are removable. (Fig. 2)

Before threading the bobbin case, wind a bobbin. Your machine will come with extra bobbins. Be sure to use the correct bobbin type made to the exact manufacturer's specifications for your machine. It is always a good idea to have plenty of extra bobbins on hand. You can purchase extras of your particular machine manufacturer's bobbins or generic types.

1

2

TIP: Plastic Bobbins vs Metal: Be sure to use a plastic bobbin in your machine if it is recommended by the manufacturer. Some bobbin mechanisms are made with magnetic parts and using metal bobbins will affect their operation. Periodically examine your bobbins for cracks or nicks; a damaged bobbin will cause stitching mishaps.

Types of Bobbins

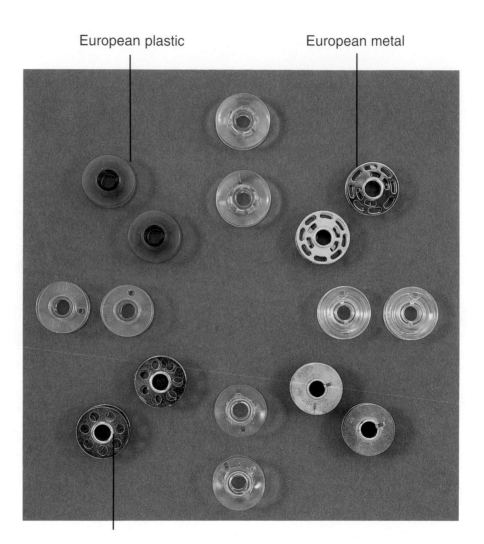

European plastic

European metal

15 class metal

HOW TO WIND A BOBBIN

The first step in winding a bobbin on a mechanical machine is to disengage the needle. This stops the needle from moving while the bobbin is winding. You can disengage the needle in one of two ways—either by releasing the clutch on the inner disk of the handwheel or by loosening the disk. To loosen the disc, hold the handwheel with one hand and turn the inside disk toward you. Consult your owner's manual for your machine's type. (Fig. 1 and 2)

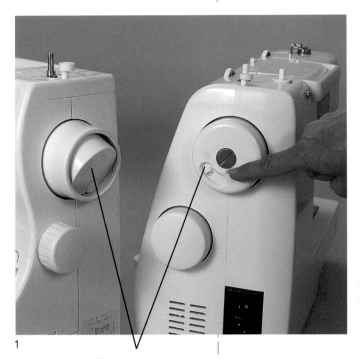

1

Releasing clutch

Loosening disk

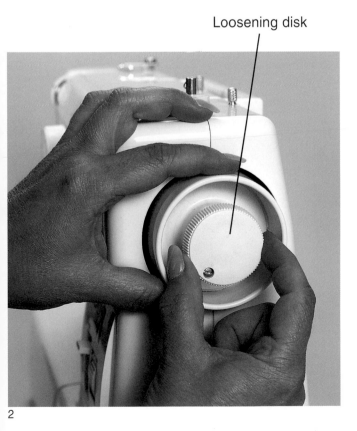

2

Computer models have a separate bobbin-winding motor that automatically stops the needle from moving once the bobbin is being wound, so it is not necessary to disengage the needle.

TIP: Use the same thread on the bobbin as the top for general stitching. For decorative stitching, use white all-purpose thread in the bobbin. It is necessary to loosen the upper tension so the white bobbin thread is kept unseen on the underside of the fabric.

Before winding the bobbin be sure that the thread is in the proper guides. This will ensure even winding. (Fig. 1 and 2) If your bobbin is wound unevenly, it will affect stitch quality and thread tension. (Fig. 3)

Side winding bobbin

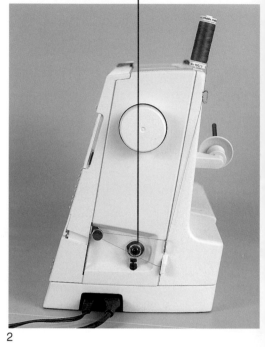

Top winding bobbin

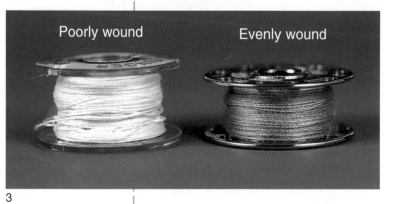

1

2

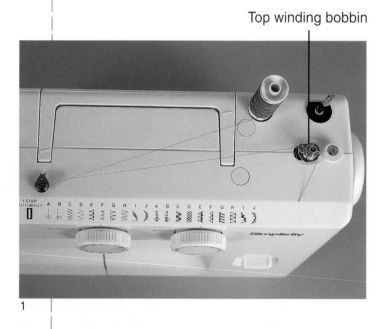

Poorly wound   Evenly wound

3

Some machines give you the option of not having to unthread the top thread when winding a bobbin. The drawback of this system is that the more thread paths and tension exerted on the thread, the more it is stretched. This may alter the stitch quality. If your stitches look uneven and/ or the fabric is puckered, wind the bobbin directly without having the upper part of the machine threaded.

After winding your bobbin, re-engage the needle by tightening the inner disc on the handwheel or declutching it.

THREADING THE BOBBIN CASE

For a drop-in bobbin case, place a full bobbin into the bobbin shuttle case with the thread going counter-clockwise (consult your owner's manual since some bobbins are fed in clockwise). While holding the bobbin down with one finger, bring the thread through the thread guide slot in the bobbin case. Pull the thread around so that it is locked into the case. You may hear a click as the thread is properly placed around the tension spring. Close the bobbin slide plate or cover. (Fig 1, 2, and 3)

1

2

3

NEEDLES
AND
THREADS

TIP: Keep your bobbins from tangling, unwinding, and rolling away. Here are several storage ideas:

Stow thread and matching bobbins together with Handi-Bobs or Bobbin Mates®. These handy bobbin holders fit into the top of a spool of thread to hold your bobbins in place with its matching thread.

Bobbin Buddies® keep bobbins from unwinding with a snap-in-place clip. Works with full or almost empty bobbins.

Another handy bobbin storage system is a bobbin box which holds up to 20 bobbins. Newer boxes have special foam grippers that cushion and hold bobbins in place and keep your bobbins tangle free. (Fig. 4)

On machines with removable bobbin cases, remove the bobbin case from the machine by lifting the latch on the outside of the case with your thumb and index finger. Use the latch to lift out the bobbin case.

To thread the bobbin case, hold the case in one hand and the wound bobbin in your thumb and index finger. (Fig. 1) Place bobbin in the case and bring the thread to the slot on the top of the case. Bring the thread down under the tension spring. Pull the thread over and around to the opening on the side of the bobbin. You may hear the thread click into place. (Fig. 2)

Replace the bobbin case into the machine using the latch on the back of the case. Be sure the case is locked into place. If the case is inserted correctly you should hear it lock into place. Close the cover. (Fig. 3)

1

2

3

4

Upper Threading

At first glance, it may appear that threading is different from machine to machine, but all threading is basically the same, passing through similar paths. Thread is fed from the spool, through thread guides, tension disks, a take-up lever and finally down to the needle. The number and style of thread guides varies from machine to machine as does the tension mechanism.

Threading a sewing machine is faster and easier than ever. Manufacturers have streamlined threading procedures with "6-second" threading, removing some of the thread guides. Others have "up-front" threading which eliminates

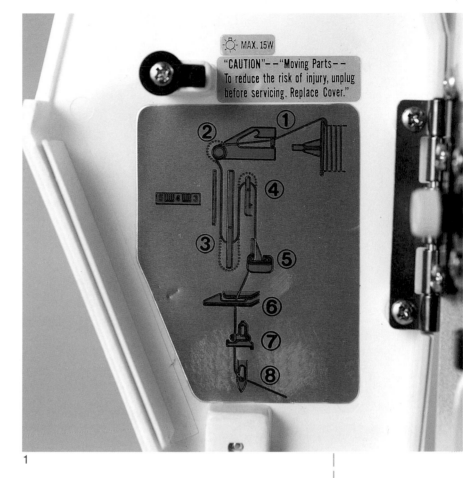

1

reaching around to the back side of the machine. Many of the newer models have threading diagrams inside the faceplate to guide you along step-by-step. (Fig. 1) When threading your machine, consult your owner's manual.

Begin by raising the presser foot which releases the tension for easy threading. (It's OK to lower the presser foot when threading the needle.) Then, bring the take-up lever to its highest point by turning the handwheel towards you. This raises the needle to its highest position and will help the thread from easily unthreading during use. On computer models, the needle will automatically stop in its highest position.

Place thread on the spool pin. For a horizontal spool pin, be sure to use the spool holder to help the thread feed smoothly. Pull thread from spool and place thread into or around the thread guides. Bring it around or between the tension disks, making sure to lock the thread down around the check spring. Then thread through the thread guides and take-up lever, remaining thread guides, and finally through the needle.

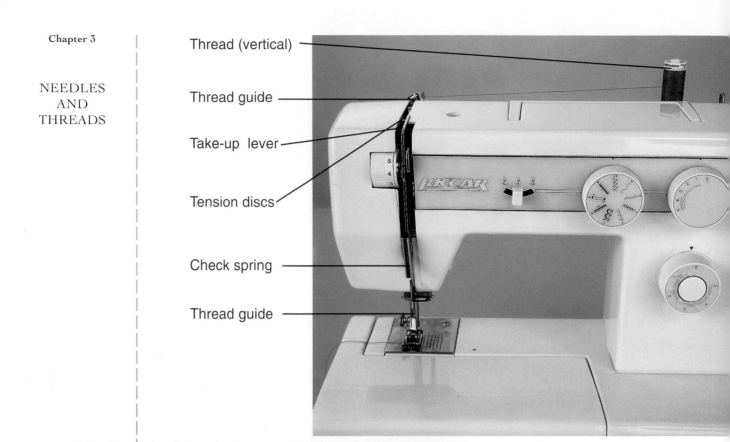

Thread (vertical)

Thread guide

Take-up lever

Tension discs

Check spring

Thread guide

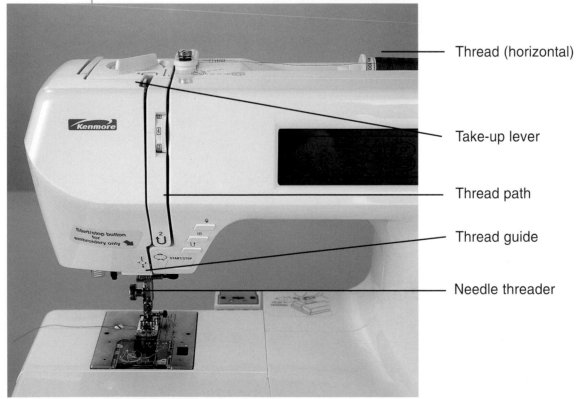

Thread (horizontal)

Take-up lever

Thread path

Thread guide

Needle threader

BRINGING UP THE BOBBIN THREAD

Before you can begin to stitch, the bobbin thread must be raised through the hole in the needle plate. First, hold the upper thread with your left hand and turn the handwheel toward you with your right hand. Lower the needle into the machine and bring it up again until a loop of the lower thread comes up through the plate. (Fig 1)

Pull on the loop of bobbin thread to draw it out and place both the top and lower threads under the presser foot. (Fig. 2) You are now ready for stitching. It is important to keep these threads at least 4" or 5" long so that they are not pulled out of the needle when brought to its highest position.

On computer models, simply tap the needle up/down position twice instead of using the handwheel to draw up the bobbin thread. Some models work by taping the foot pedal twice to drop the needle and bring it up again.

Note: Some machines have an automatic thread take-up which eliminates having to draw up the thread before you can begin sewing. Consult your owner's manual.

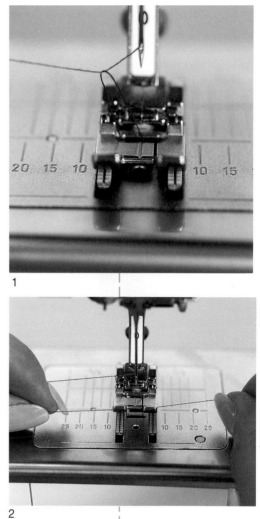

1

2

The Tension Is Building

When I was learning to sew, my teacher instructed us "never to touch the tension," but I often wondered what this mysterious dial could do. Sewers often claim that tension is the one feature on their sewing machine that gives them the most stress. Actually, that is exactly what a tension device is supposed to do (to the thread not you). Its function is to extend or maintain tension on the thread as it passes through the machine.

Tension is the most misunderstood feature in machine operation, but it is not so complicated once you understand its theory. Knowing how your machine tension works will allow you to fine-tune your stitching for the fabric and application desired. The tension control determines the amount of pressure on the threads. Too much pressure causes too little thread being fed into the stitch thus causing a puckered stitch. Too little pressure feeds through too much thread and causes a weak, loose stitch.

NEEDLES
AND
THREADS

Upper-thread tension controls are on every machine and most have a bobbin thread tension as well. These controls increase or decrease the pressure or strain exerted on the thread as it is fed through the machine. (Fig. 1) Just as with the top tension, too much or too little tension on the bobbin will result in puckering, threads breaking, and a weak seam. When tension is correctly set on both top and bobbin, a balanced stitch will be the result.

Tension dials are on the machine for you to use. For the most part, once your tension is correctly set, you will rarely need to adjust it for "normal" stitching applications. It is important to note that the "correct" tension setting will not be the same for all machines. Settings will vary from brand to brand and model to model. (Fig. 2 and 3) Generally, you will need to make a slight tension adjustment when zigzag stitching and again for satin stitching. Some machines automatically adjust tension for specific stitches. Others indicate the correct setting with a marking right on the dial. Consult your owner's manual for assistance.

Before starting to sew on a new fabric or when using a new stitch function, it is always a good idea to perfect the stitch on fabric scraps first. Use the same fabric and number of layers you will be sewing and the correct needle and thread. Set the stitch length on 2.5mm–3mm or 10–12 stitches per inch (s/p/i). Make a stitch sample, examine it carefully, make any necessary adjustment, then test again.

Tension disk

1

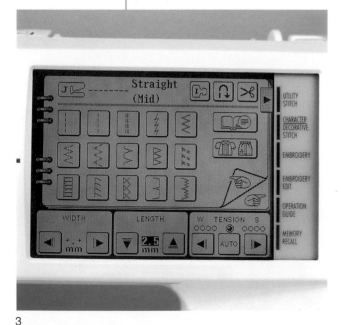

3

2

The **correct tension** should look balanced on both sides of the fabric layers. The stitch should lock the top and bottom threads in the middle of the fabric. The stitches are even in length and the tension is even on both sides of the fabric. The fabric lies flat and is not pulled or puckered.

A **too-tight tension** shows that the bottom thread is pulling up to the top side of the fabric. The fabric is puckered and the stitch easily can be broken. The stitches also may appear uneven in length. This problem is due to either too much tension on the top thread, or too little on the bobbin thread. To correct, decrease the top tension.

A **too-loose tension** shows the top thread is being pulled down to the bottom side of the fabric layers. The seam is weak and will pull apart. To correct this problem, tighten the tension.

TIP: When testing your machine's tension balance, thread the upper thread in a different color than the bobbin. This will help you quickly determine which tension adjustments need to be made.

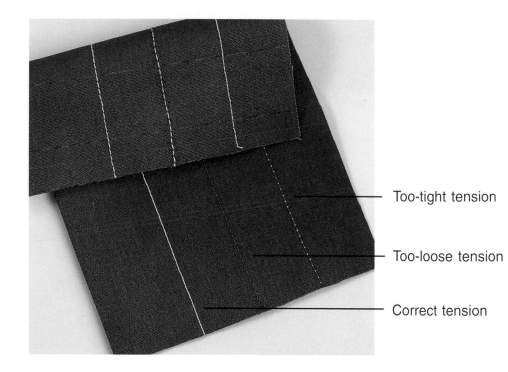

— Too-tight tension

— Too-loose tension

— Correct tension

TIP: Once you've perfected your stitch, note the correct tension, stitch length, and pressure setting, on your test sample and place it in a notebook or your owner's manual. This way you'll have it for future reference.

The Tension Test

Test your seam by cutting a 6" square of fabric. Fold the fabric on the bias (diagonal) and stitch ½" from the fold. Does the line of stitching pucker? Is the stitch balanced on the top and bottom of the fabric?

To determine if the tension is correct, hold the ends of the fabric between your thumb and index finger at the end of the stitching line. Pull on the stitching with an even quick force until one thread breaks. If the needle thread broke, the upper tension is too loose. If both threads broke together and if it took a considerable force to break them, the tensions are balanced. (Fig. 1)

1

How to Adjust the Upper Tension

The tension regulator dial is located either on top or close to the tension disks and will indicate the amount of tension the dial is set for. Adjust this control with your machine threaded and the presser foot down (tension is released when the presser foot is up). To decrease the tension, turn the dial down or to a lower number. To increase tension, turn the dial to a higher number. (Fig. 1)

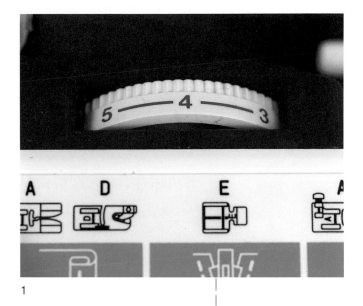

1

The Bobbin Tension

When a stitch tension cannot be balanced correctly by adjusting upper tension, it may be necessary to adjust the bobbin thread tension. The bobbin tension is adjusted with a screw located on the tension spring of the bobbin case; some have one screw while others have two. (A bobbin case can be removable or built-in the machine.) (Fig. 2)) Before adjusting this tension screw, thread the bobbin. Using the tiny screwdriver that came with your machine, carefully turn the screw with only minute turns. A quarter of a turn may even be too much. To tighten the tension, turn the screw to the right or clockwise; to loosen, turn the screw to the left or counterclockwise. To remember this, I always repeat: rightly tightly, lefty loosely. (Fig. 3)

2

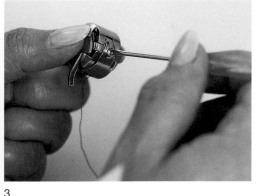

3

Caution: The bobbin tension screw is tiny and can be lost easily. Be sure to make only small turns when adjusting. With a removable bobbin case, hold the case over a piece of white paper or a box when making adjustments so if the screw is dropped, it can be found easily.

Testing Bobbin Tension

Test your removable bobbin tension by holding the thread tail of the threaded bobbin and letting the case dangle. Give the thread a jerk. Does the case slip down? Or, does the thread support the weight of the bobbin and case. If not, tighten the screw a quarter to a half turn.

The Pressure's On

The presser foot pressure also can alter a stitch. Pressure is the force the presser foot exerts on the fabric and the feed dogs when stitching. Pressure is important because it regulates how the machine feeds the fabric layers. The correct pressure will feed the fabric through straight and even. Generally, pressure is set at its full pressure or highest number for "normal" stitching. The higher the number, the more the pressure. Some regulators are pop-up styles or screw types, and do not have number indicators for their settings. Consult your owner's manual for correct settings.

When do you adjust the pressure? When a stitch is puckered or when stitching napped, fine, and heavy-weight fabrics, knits, the presser foot may require fine-tuning. If the fabric puckers or when it appears wavy, the pressure regulator needs to be decreased or set at a lower number. Increase the pressure when stitching thick fabrics and multiple layers as well as fine silkies. Knit fabrics will stretch out of shape with too much presser foot pressure, so decrease the pressure. It also may be necessary to lighten the pressure when doing decorative stitches.

SEAM FINISHES (Continued)

6. **Bound Seam**
that ravel easi[...]
or coats. Sti[...]
open. Encase[...]
tape. Baste;[...]
nesses, as sh[...]
pressed on[...]

7. **Turned**
line[...]

6. Bound Seam

7. Turned and Stitched E[...]

8. Turned Edges Stitched Togeth[...]

9. Double Stitched Seam

10. Rol[...]

THE
RY FRANCES
VING BOOK

EOPLE

CONTENTS · MERC[...]
Postmaster:Thisparcelmaybeopenedforpo[...]
THE OHIO[...]
PATTERN D[...]
243 WEST 17th STRE[...]
RETURN POS[...]

► JAV[...]
JU[...]
SAVE PINS

DETAIL INSTR[...]

GETTING DOWN TO THE BASICS

By now, you have familiarized yourself with the parts of your machine and the important components of needles and thread. You've learned how to thread your machine from top to bottom and you're ready to sew!

TIP: Maintaining good posture while at your machine will help you work more comfortably. Sit back on your chair and lean forward slightly. Position your body squarely in front of the needle.

Straight Stitch Fundamentals

This chapter will concentrate on straight-stitch fundamentals, including topstitching; how to make a beautiful buttonhole; and basic utility stitches and how they are used.

To start, a straight stitch is the basis of all sewing. A good straight stitch is the difference between a professional finished project and one of an amateur. The goal here is to get a prefect straight stitch, then everything else will be a breeze.

If this is your first experience venturing into operating a sewing machine, allow yourself some practice time. When I was in school learning to sew, we began stitching on sheets of lined paper — no thread, just the needle and lined paper. Begin by following the printed lines to practice stitching straight. Work on keeping the machine's speed evenly controlled. My sewing teacher always said "a good sewer is a slow sewer" and to this day I hear myself repeating these words. If your machine has a speed control, begin by setting it in the mid-range. Use the high speed for long straight stitching when you feel comfortable with your machine.

When you've mastered straight-line stitching, take a piece of white paper and draw boxes (lines with corners), curves, and circles. These take a bit more skill to keep the stitches straight but take your time and practice. To turn a corner, lower the needle into the paper or fabric exactly where you want to turn, raise the presser foot, and pivot the paper (fabric) 90°. Lower the presser foot and continue stitching. This technique will come in handy when stitching pockets, collars, lapels, necklines, and much more.

Curved areas tend to be tricky, but with slow stitching, they too, can be mastered. Guide the paper on small curves by stopping with the needle in the fabric and lifting the presser foot slightly and turn the paper just enough to follow the curve.

Practice on fabric scraps when you are ready. Another good exercise is guiding the edge of the fabric along the seam guide markings on the needle and slide plate. This will keep the stitching parallel to the fabric's cut edge for a straight seam of consistent width.

Fully adjustable stitch length selectors are on most machines. It is essential to use the correct stitch length even for straight stitching. Stitch length is selected based on fabric weight, texture, and structure. The most important consideration is the fabric's weight. The heavier the fabric, the longer the stitch; the lighter the fabric, the shorter the stitch.

The fabric's texture and structure also needs consideration. A normal stitch length for most medium-weight fabrics is 2.5mm or 10–12 s/p/i. (Computer machines will automatically be set at this stitch length when the machine is turned on. You can override this feature and set the desired length.) Velvet is a soft fabric, but has a nap and requires a stitch length of 2mm–2.5mm. Crepe also is a soft fabric and looks best with a stitch length of 2.0mm. Knit fabrics may require a shorter stitch length of 1.5mm–2mm. A longer stitch is recommended for leather, denims, vinyl and the like. There is always a stitch length range for every fabric, and it is best to test various stitch lengths on a fabric scrap before beginning any new project.

In general, when stitching fine or soft fabrics, set the stitch length on 2mm–2.5mm. For medium- to heavy-weight fabric, use a length of 3mm–3.5mm to prevent puckering. A basting stitch is a length of 4mm or the longest stitch available on the machine. When gathering, the longest stitch length is used, and for easing, a length of 4mm is best.

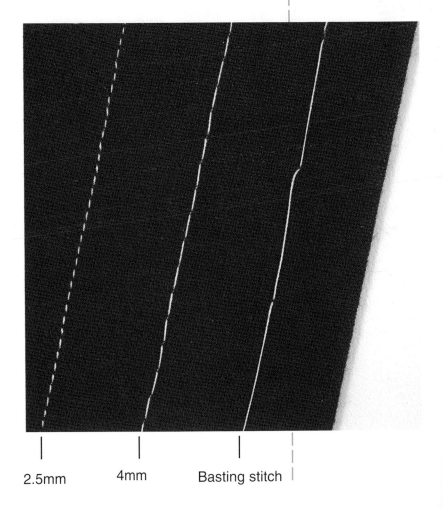

2.5mm   4mm   Basting stitch

Stitch-length Selectors

Most stitch-length selectors are based on the metric numbers from 0 up to 6 — 6 meaning a very long stitch used for basting and decreasing as the numbers go down. A normal stitch for seaming is set at 2.5mm. Older machines indicate stitch length based on the imperial number system with number of stitches per inch — 18–20 s/p/i being the longest and 6 s/p/i the shortest. (Fig. 1, 2 and 3)

Most machines have a reverse control and will sew in reverse at about the same length as they did when stitching forward.

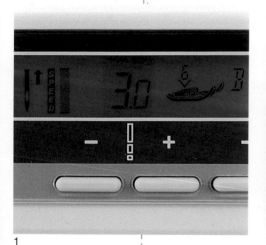

1

2

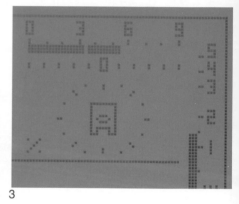

3

Keeping Your Straight-Stitch Straight

Tips for a perfect stitch:

- Before stitching, prepare fabric by pressing it flat and smooth.
- Use the correct needle size and type.
- Change the needle before beginning a new project.
- Use the same quality and color thread in both the top and in the bobbin.
- Do a stitch sample on a fabric scrap first to be sure all settings are perfect for your fabric.
- After stitching, press again to set the line of stitching. Allow to cool before handling.

How to Start and End a Seam

1. Raise the take-up lever to its highest point by turning the handwheel toward you.

2. Bring both top and bobbin thread under the presser foot and place them behind or to the side of the foot.

3. Position the fabric under the presser foot ½" from the back edge, having the bulk of fabric to the left and the cut edge along the seam guide on the needle plate markings. (Fig. 1)

4. Begin by taking a few back stitches to secure the seam. Continue stitching forward at a slow consistent speed.

5. When you reach the end of the seam, backstitch again to reinforce the seam. Bring the take-up lever to its highest point and raise the presser foot. Cut the threads using the machine's thread cutter or a scissors.

1

CREATIVE WAYS TO STRAIGHT STITCH

Decorative thread gives straight stitching a new look. Use it to make expensive-looking fabric coordinates. Experiment with straight stitching. Try running rows of stitches between stripes, on the squares of a plaid, or create an all-over design. Embellish just part of a garment, like a collar or cuffs, with this method.

Create a firm tapestry-like fabric by covering a plain fabric with closely spaced rows of decorative stitches sewn with decorative thread. Or, stitch an outline around a print motif with a shiny thread for a mock appliqué look.

TIP: When stitching, do not push or pull the fabric. This will cause the needle to break under the stress. You only need to guide the fabric in front of the presser foot while stitching. Let the machine's feed dog's do the work. For difficult fabrics, such as silkies and knits, it may be necessary to gently hold the seam taut in front and in back of the presser foot.

TIP: Prevent skipped stitches when stitching from 2 fabric layers to 4 or 6. Set your machine for a long stitch length (3.5mm or 6 s/p/i) and use a denim needle. Attach a roller foot and as the foot tips up on the seam, push down on the toe as you stitch over the thick layers. This will help keep the foot and feed dogs working together.

TIP: Here's a quick tip for shirring a single layer of fabric using a straight stitch. Attach a standard buttonhole foot or open-toe embroidery foot. Tighten the upper tension to its highest number and set stitch length for a long basting stitch. Place fabric under the presser foot and begin stitching. As you stitch, hold your index finger directly behind the presser foot. This will cause the fabric to pile up and gather as you stitch. Use this technique to ease sleeve caps and any place where soft gathers are called for.

Trouble-shooting Check Points

Don't let stitching problems get the best of you. In my experience I've discovered, much to my dismay, that most of my stitching problems are due to operator fault, not machine fault. If you are having stitching difficulties, refer to this checklist for help.

The needle — If your needle is bent, burred, dull, or simply the wrong size or type, this will cause many stitching snafus. It may not be obvious to the eye but the tinniest little burr can wreak havoc with your machine. When in doubt, insert a new needle.

Threading — Is the machine correctly threaded? Often, in haste, I incorrectly thread my machine, skipping a thread guide or totally missing the take-up lever. It is also common for the thread to slip out of the take-up lever or tension disks while stitching. Unthread both the top and bottom threads then rethread.

The thread — Inexpensive thread brands tend to shred, leaving behind fibers in the machine that will eventually buildup and cause problems. Try using different thread brands to find out what works best for your machine. Use a good quality thread.

Is your machine due for a cleaning? — Before beginning a new project, it is a good idea to inspect your machine. With a tiny lint brush, remove any thread, lint or dust from your machine following the manual's instructions. Oil your machine if it is needed or overdue (and if your machine requires it) and always consult the machine's manual for instructions.

Topstitching

This seemingly simple detail must be perfect, whether it is one row of edgestitching or multiple rows of straight stitching. For best results, here are some tips to use for perfectly straight topstitching and creative ways to apply your newfound skill.

- Use a new needle and select a thread compatible to your fabric's weight.

- Loosen your top tension slightly to be sure the bobbin thread is pulled more to the underside of the fabric.

- Use a seam guide which is fully adjustable and can be screwed into the bed of the machine; magnetic seam guides are also available. (**Note:** Some magnetic seam guides are not recommended for use on computerized machines.) Set the guide the desired distance from the needle and align the fabric next to the guide for perfectly straight rows of topstitching. Or, create your own guide with a strip of masking tape placed on your machines needle plate in the desired position.

- A topstitching foot with an adjustable guide will prevent fabric from slipping while stitching. The blindhem foot that came with your machine can be used as a topstitching guide. Your machine's overedge foot also may have a guide that will work. Adjust the needle position to place your stitching where desired.

- An even-feed or walking foot is a great topstitching aid when working on layers of fabric. Use it with a seam guide for straight rows.

- A quilting foot works when a perfect ¼" topstitch is desired. Simply place the fabric edge even with the foot's edge. Use the markings on the foot for pivoting around a corner a perfect ¼".

- A quilting guide can be used to stitch evenly spaced rows of topstitching.

- When top-stitching thick fabrics, the standard presser foot sometimes gets stuck. Use a walking foot or even-feed foot to help feed the top and bottom layers evenly and move the fabric along smoothly. A roller foot or a Teflon™ coated foot also keeps the layers from shifting and lessens the "drag" against the under side of the all-purpose foot.

CREATIVE WAYS TO USE TOPSTITCHING

- Select a longer stitch length for a bolder look. Lightweight fabrics may call for a shorter stitch to avoid puckering. For subtle detail, use matching thread. For a noticeable effect choose a contrasting thread.
- Use topstitching to echo design lines of a garment. Or, mimic a fabric's print and outline a floral motif or geometric pattern. Use a layer of filler between the garment and lining for a raised topstitched effect. For a fuller effect, use fleece for padding and for a subtle effect use a layer of flannel or cotton fabric as the filler.
- For more distinct topstitching, use 2 threads in 1 needle. Place a filled bobbin on the upper thread spool and thread machine as usual. Use a topstitching needle, with its large eye, making it easier to thread the needle with 2 threads.
- Use the edge of the presser foot between rows for evenly spaced rows.
- Instead of using a straight stitch, try a narrow zigzag or satin stitch.
- A twin needle makes decorative topstitching in half the time. Use matching or contrasting thread in each needle.
- When topstitching, don't backstitch. To secure end of stitch, pull top thread to the underside and secure with a knot.
- When stitching around curves, loosen the presser foot pressure to make it easier to pull the fabric around as you stitch. Practice on a scrap of fabric before stitching on actual project.
- Stitch slowly and take your time.

Twin Needle Stitching

Twin needles have 2 needles on 1 crossbar mounted to a single shank. When used they make 2 parallel rows of stitching in 1 step. The bobbin thread produces a zigzag on the underside. Twin needles range in size from 1.6/70 to 6.0/100. Their numbering system indicates first the space between the needles, then the needle size. Be sure to choose a size suitable for your fabric and to consider the needle spacing when setting the machine's stitch width.

Use a twin needle to secure a hem, topstitch a collar or create a decorative detail. Experiment with the stitches on your machine. Even a simple zigzag stitch will take on a whole new appearance when sewn with a twin needle. For more decorative interest, use 2 different color threads on top.

Using A Twin Needle

Thread machine with 2 spools of thread on top (stack a bobbin on top of a spool of thread if you don't have an extra spool pin). Follow the normal threading path with both threads on your machine. Place the spools so they unwind in opposite directions to prevent knotting. At the tension, place 1 thread on the left side of the disk and 1 on the other. (Fig. 1) Some machines have a thread guide just before the needle that allows you to separate the threads. Place 1 thread in the left guide and 1 in the right guide. If your machine has only one guide, thread 1 in the guide and leave the other out. (Fig. 2) Be sure to use a zigzag needle plate.

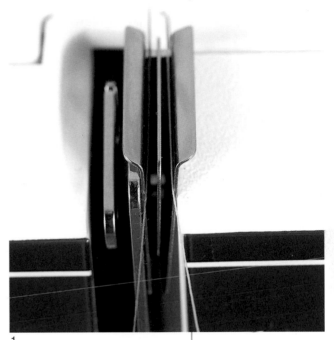

1

Before stitching, manually turn the handwheel to make sure the needles clear the presser foot and needle plate. This is important especially when using a zigzag stitch. Note: Some computer machines have a twin-needle safety button; this is usually for a 2.0 or smaller twin needle. To use a wider width needle, reset the stitch width manually to a *narrower* setting.

To stitch corners, stop with the needles down, raise the presser foot, and pivot the fabric halfway around the corner, then lower the presser foot. Manually turn the handwheel taking 1 stitch to be sure the inner needle stitches are correctly placed. Leave the needle down, raise the presser foot and pivot the fabric again to compete the corner. Continue stitching.

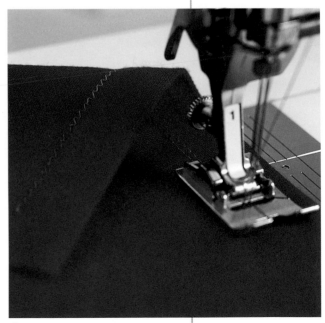

2

TIP: If your machine has only 1 spool pin, use a drinking straw to extend the length of a vertical spool pin. Trim the straw to desired length; this way you can place a second spool of thread over the first.

TIP: When stitching with twin and triple needles, stitch slowly. This will help produce more consistent stitching.

DOUBLE-STITCHED HEM

A double-stitch hem is decorative and functional when a twin-needle stitch is used. Because the bobbin produces a flexible zigzag on the underside of the fabric, twin-needle stitching prevents the hem from rolling and adds elasticity to the straight-stitched hem. It is the perfect stitch for knits.

Press up the hem and stitch as usual. As you stitch, the bobbin thread spans the twin needles, adding stretch to the finished stitch. It may be helpful to loosen the bobbin tension if a ridge occurs between the two rows of straight stitches. Trim the hem allowance close to the stitching.

Triple Needle Stitching

A triple needle stitches 3 parallel rows for a 3mm-wide stitch. Use it for hemming and decorative topstitching. Thread the machine with 2 spools just as you would for twin-needle stitching. Wind an extra bobbin for the third spool. Place this bobbin under the left spool and place the thread through the center needle.

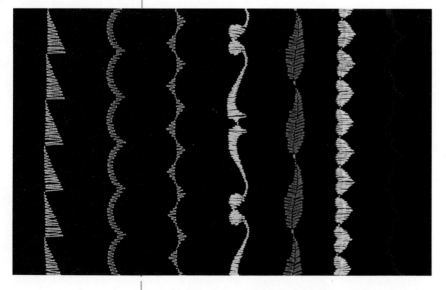

The Versatile Zigzag Stitch

Both functional and decorative, the zigzag is a versatile stitch that you will use again and again. A zigzag is a lockstitch with a side-to-side width. The stitch length can be altered for various end results. A zigzag stitch has more give than a straight stitch, so it has more flexibility. A very narrow zigzag stitch can be used for sewing stretch fabrics for less breakage. When zigzag stitching, use a zigzag foot and needle plate (if a separate one is given). The zigzag foot has a tunnel or cutout underneath it to allow it to smoothly pass over the stitches.

The length and width of the zigzag changes the end result. The stitch length and width will depend on your purposes: a narrow width setting is used for seaming stretchy fabrics; for edge-finishing, a medium width and short length creates a satin-stitch edge and is best on fabric that is very ravely; and a multi-stitch zigzag is suggested for edge-finishing frayed fabrics. A shorter and wider multi-stitch zigzag is used for mending or can be used decoratively in a fagotted seam.

Tension Settings for the Zigzag Stitch

For a balanced zigzag stitch, the interlocking top and bottom threads should fall at the corner of each stitch and midway between the fabric layers. When the tension is incorrect, the stitch tends to draw up the fabric and cause puckering.

Correct zigzag tension—Balanced threads are linked at the sides of each zigzag stitch. The fabric is flat.

Too tight—The bottom thread is being pulled up toward the top fabric layer; and the fabric may be puckered. To correct, decrease the top tension or (only if this doesn't work) increase the bobbin tension.

Too loose—The top thread will be pulled to the underside of the fabric and the fabric may be puckered. Increase the top tension. If this doesn't work, decrease the bobbin tension.

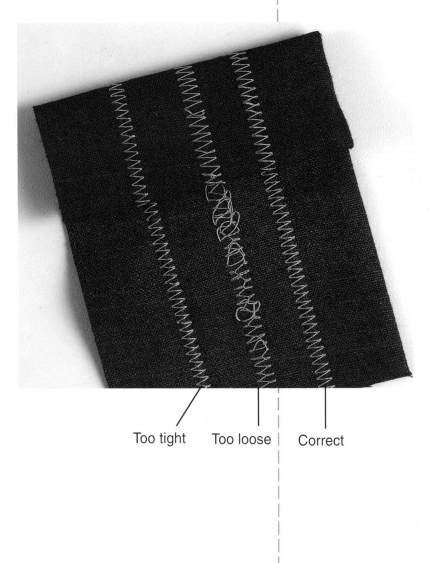

Too tight   Too loose   Correct

Uses for the Zigzag

Put your zigzag stitch to work. Here are some practical and decorative uses for the versatile zigzag.

1

—NARROW ZIGZAG SEAMS

A narrow zigzag stitch can be used to seam knit fabrics. Set stitch width at 1mm–1.5mm and length at 1.5mm–2mm. Hold the fabric taut as you stitch. Press seam flat, then press open. (Fig. 1)

—EDGE FINISHING

Stitch over the edge of loosely woven fabrics to minimize fraying. If the edge is puckering use an overcast foot or use a stabilizer under the fabric. Set stitch width at 3mm–4mm and length at 1mm–1.5mm (adjust according to your fabric). Attach satin stitch foot or embroidery foot. Place the cut edge of fabric under the foot half way so that the needle falls off the fabric as it swings to the right. (If the fabric begins to tunnel under the stitch use an overcast foot to keep it flat.) (Fig. 2)

For a turn and stitch finish like those on casings, overcast using a zigzag.

2

—GATHERING

A quick and easy way to gather a long piece of fabric is to zigzag over a piece of cord. Use pearl cotton or buttonhole twist, even dental floss (unwaxed) will work. Set stitch width at 3mm–4mm and a 2mm–3mm stitch length. Place fabric under the foot and place cord just inside the seamline. Zigzag over the cord making sure you do not stitch through it. Knot one end to secure and pull up on remaining end to gather. (Fig. 1 and 2)

1

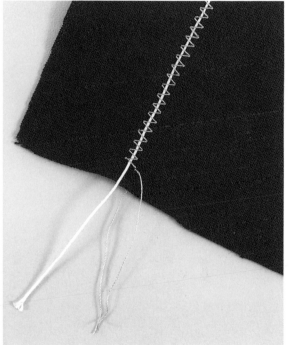

2

—ELASTIC APPLICATION

The zigzag stitch is used to attach elastic by stitching through it or by making a casing for narrow elastic for children's and doll clothes.

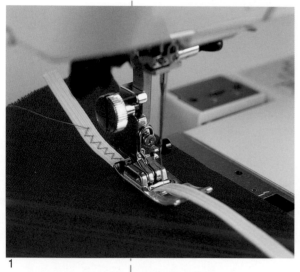

1

2

Stitching through elastic—Set machine for a wide 3mm–4mm zigzag and 2mm–3mm stitch length. Attach satin-stitch or embroidery foot. Place fabric under the foot and the elastic under the groove of the presser foot. Pass the elastic through the slot so it is resting on the center portion of the foot. Carefully zigzag over the elastic, stretching it as you stitch. It is helpful to anchor the elastic in several places with a pin before stitching. (Fig. 1 and 2)

To make an elastic casing—Set machine for a wide 4mm–5mm zigzag stitch and a long stitch length. Attach satin-stitch or embroidery foot. Slide elastic under the foot and up through the slot on the presser foot so it is resting on top of the center portion. Insert fabric under foot with the wrong side up (the elastic is attached to the inside). Stitch gently pulling elastic as you go making sure you are stitching over, not through, the elastic. Secure ends of elastic with a straight stitch. (Fig. 3 and 4)

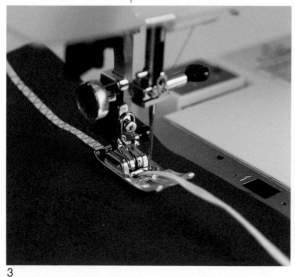

3

4

—ATTACHING A BUTTON

Flat, sew-through buttons can quickly and securely be attached to a garment by machine using a zigzag stitch. Use your machine's button sew-on foot or remove the presser foot completely (the sew-on foot helps hold the button in place while stitching). Place garment and button under the presser foot. (Fig. 1) Use clear transparent tape to hold button in place and remove tape after stitching. Lower or use the special plate to cover the feed dogs (you don't want the machine to move forward when stitching a button). Set your machine for a zigzag stitch and adjust the width by dropping the needle into the left hole of the button turning the handwheel and making sure the needle spans the holes in the button.

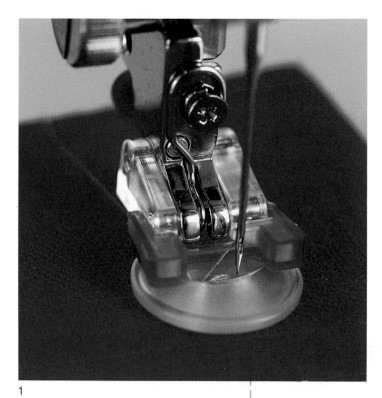

1

2

To create a thread shank, place a straight pin or toothpick over the button or use the button reed (Fig. 2) accessory provided with your machine. Stitch over the pin several times to secure the button to the garment. To lock stitches, set width at "0" and take several stitches in one place. Cut threads and leave long ends then bring ends between button and fabric. Wrap ends around the thread shank and tie a knot. Use seam sealant to secure knot.

—SATIN STITCHING

As an edge finish, use a satin stitch to simulate a serger rolled hem on napkins, table-cloths, and ruffles. Set machine for a narrow 2.0mm width and 0.5mm stitch length. Attach the satin-stitch foot or embroidery foot. For a more filled-in look use embroidery thread. Place the right side of the fabric under the machine's presser foot so that the edge is centered. Begin stitching, allowing the needle to go off the fabric's edge when it swings to the right. If desired, use this technique as a hem finish, folding the hem under and stitching along the fold. Trim excess fabric on the underside close to the stitching. (Fig. 1 and 2)

—APPLIQUÉ STITCH

A satin stitch is used to create a smooth, satin-like finish for decorative purposes. For more information on how to appliqué see the information given in Chapter 5, Decorative Stitch Options.

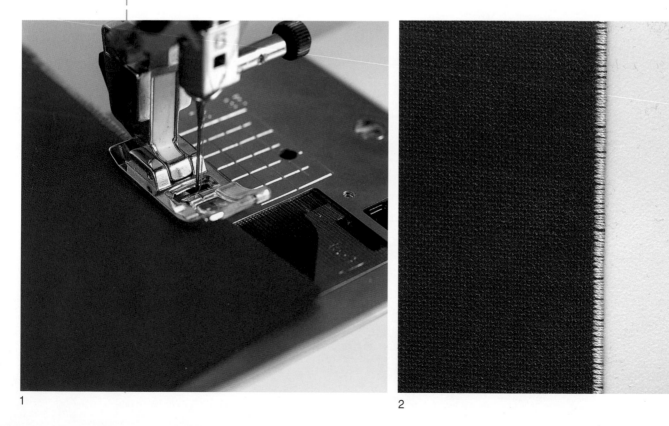

1

2

—BUTTON AND BELT LOOPS

By stitching over pearl cotton or multiple strands of thread (to match your garment), you can create beautiful button and belt loops. For button loops with give, use round elastic thread as your filler. Set your machine at its widest zigzag and a 0.5mm stitch length. Use an embroidery foot or satin-stitch foot. A standard buttonhole foot with a notch on back for cording also will work. Place pearl cotton or thread strands under and behind the presser foot (or around notch of buttonhole foot). Hold the top and bobbin thread tails behind the foot and stitch over the core thread so the stitches cover it. (Fig. 1) To attach to garment use a tapestry needle to hand stitch in place.

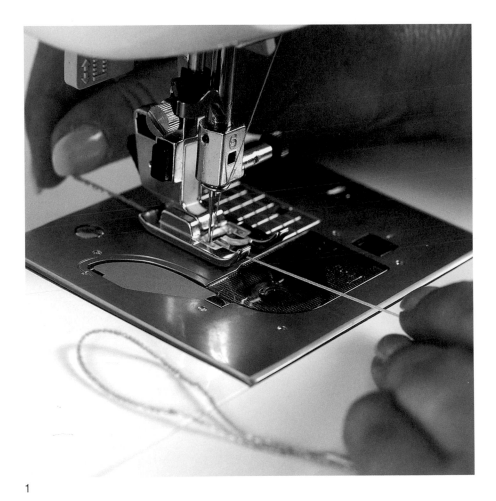

1

—ZIGZAG OVER CORD

Use a strand or 2 of pearl cotton or topstitching thread under your satin stitching as a filler to give the stitch a raised effect. Set your machine for a 2mm–4mm width and a 0.5 stitch length. Attach an embroidery foot or satin-stitch foot. A cording foot may be helpful to guide the cord. Place the cord under the back of the presser foot and up through the slot on the foot so it is resting on top of the center portion. Or, insert cord under center slot of cording foot. Place the fabric under the foot so the cord is aligned with the cut edge. Satin-stitch along the edge so that when the needle swings to the right, it is off the fabric's edge. If needed, place a tear-away stabilizer under fabric. At a corner, pivot the fabric, making a loop in the cord. Continue stitching for 1", then pull up on the cord to eliminate the loop. (Fig. 1 and 2) To end, cut the filler cord and overlap the stitching to secure.

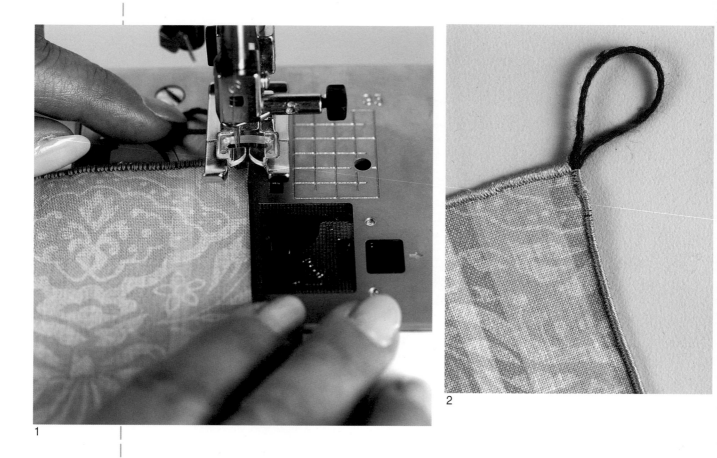

1

2

—COUCHING

This technique is where cording is attached to an item with a long zigzag stitch. The stitches are over, not through, the cord. Use this technique with string, cord, yarn, flat trims, and ribbon floss. The decorative cord will show and be part of the design. Try blending thread and cording colors by loosely twisting several strands together and zigzagging over them.

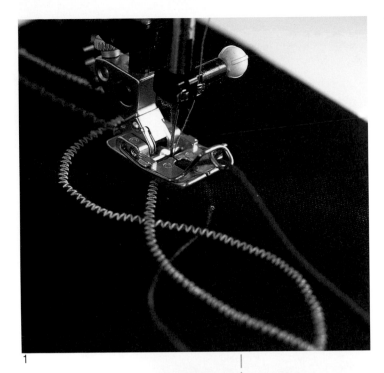

Set your machine for a 3mm–4mm width (or wide enough to stitch over the cord) and a 1mm–2mm stitch length. Attach an embroidery, standard buttonhole foot, or cording foot. Use decorative thread or a monofilament thread for an invisible stitch. Mark the position for couching. Place the cord under the back of the presser foot and up through the slot on the presser foot so it is resting on top of the center portion. Stitch, allowing the zigzag stitches to go over the cord. Guide the cord, following your markings. (Fig. 1)

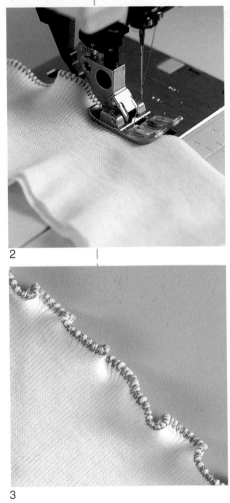

—LETTUCE EDGE

Create ripples on the edge of stretch fabrics or the bias as you stretch the fabric while stitching it. This technique is often seen as a hem finish on children's garments.

Set machine for a 3mm–5mm width and 0.5–1mm stitch length. Attach an embroidery or satin-stitch foot. Place the fabric's folded edge under the presser foot, right side up.

Hold the fabric in front of and behind the presser foot and stretch it as you stitch. Allow the needle to swing off the fabric's edge as it swings to the right. For a more filled-in look, stitch over your first row again. (Fig. 2 and 3)

Variations On The Zigzag Stitch — Buttonholes

Sewing machine technology has led buttonhole making in an entirely new direction. Today's sewers need not fear the buttonhole. Most machines have built-in buttonholers that are easy enough to master with a little practice.

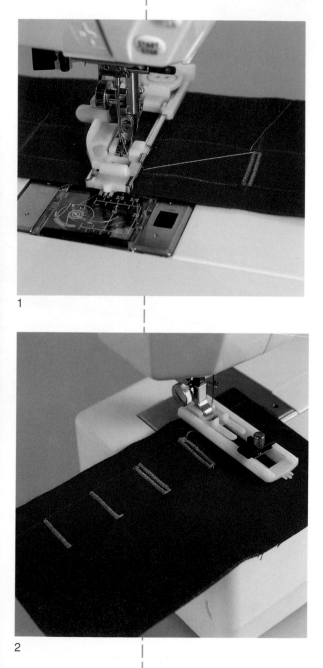

1

2

Machine-made buttonholes can be done automatically in 1 step or up to 4 steps. One-step buttonholes are available on computer models. Simply place your button in the special sliding buttonhole foot and attach to your machine. A lever is usually pulled down or a sensor is built into the foot that actually tells the computer the exact size of your button for the perfectly sized buttonhole. There's no need to measure the buttonhole size; simply mark the placement on your garment. Most computer machines can be overridden so you can manually size your buttonholes as well as control the density of the zigzag. (Fig. 1)

Four-step buttonholes make a buttonhole with a forward zigzag stitch, a bar tack, a reverse zigzag and a finishing bar-tack stitch. (Fig. 2) A 2-step combines the forward or backward zigzag with a bar tack. There is no need to pivot, change needle position, or turn your fabric. The buttonhole stitching steps are indicated right on the machine's dial or lever. Before stitching, you will have to manually set the stitch length and width which are usually clearly marked on the machine with a special color code. Before stitching these styles, mark the fabric the proper buttonhole length as your starting and stopping points.

Note: Some mechanical machines also have balance adjustments; consult your owner's manual. Be careful not to adjust your tension to balance your buttonhole.

Buttonhole Feet

A sliding buttonhole foot has a button holder on the back of the foot to insert your button and determine the buttonhole length. Buttonholes can be made in sizes from ¼" to 1¼" in length. To use this foot, simply slide and lock the button in place (some have a locking screw and others do not). As the machine stitches the buttonhole, it is sized for the button. These feet have a long base and will hold your fabric in place securely while stitching. (Fig. 1)

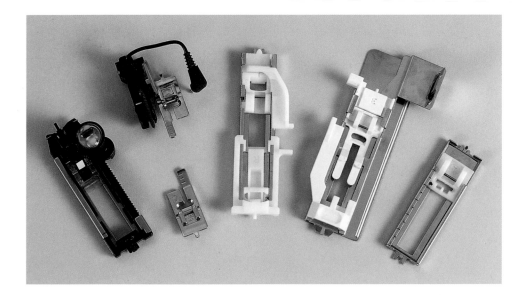

The standard buttonhole foot is used when a large button doesn't fit into a sliding buttonhole foot or when positioning the sliding foot is awkward. It is designed with narrow channels on the heel of the underside of the foot. This foot may also have a raised notch on the back or front end for corded buttonholes. There are many other uses for this foot, as mentioned throughout this chapter. (Fig. 1)

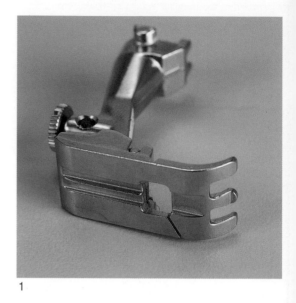

1

For accurate buttonhole placement begin stitching horizontal buttonholes at the marking closest to the garment edge. Begin stitching vertical buttonholes at the marking closest to the upper edge of the garment.

If your machine does not measure the buttonhole size automatically, make buttonholes ⅛" larger than your button. If your button is thick, increase the size of your buttonhole a little. Do a test sample before making buttonhole on your garment.

Always make a test buttonhole on a fabric scarp before stitching the actual garment. Be sure to use the same number of fabric layers, including interfacing, as the garment. Cut the buttonhole open to check the size.

2

Place a strip of ⅛"-wide transparent tape or masking tape along one side of your buttonhole markings. Stitch next to the tape for a straight buttonhole. (Fig. 2)

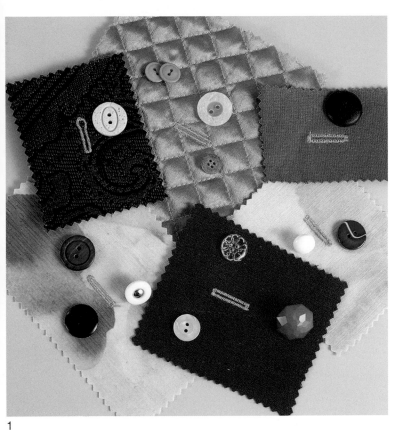

1

TIP: To add strength to a buttonhole and to make it look corded, stitch over it twice using a narrower and slightly longer stitch length first.

Buttonhole Styles

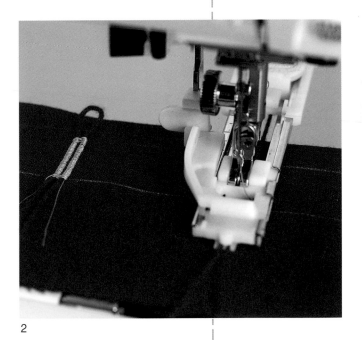

2

Corded buttonholes—Used to prevent stretching and gaping. Stitch over a fine cord (topstitching thread) for reinforcement using the notched cord guide on the buttonhole foot. After stitching buttonhole, pull the thread ends to hide the loop. Knot the thread ends and bring them to the wrong side by threading them through a tapestry needle. (Fig. 2)

Rounded buttonhole—Used for shirts and blouses of fine fabric. One or both ends can be rounded. (Fig. 1)

Keyhole buttonhole—Used for men's jackets and tailored garments, coats, slacks, and jeans. It has an eyelet to accommodate a shank button. (Fig. 1)

Knit Buttonhole—Lays fewer stitches on knit fabric to eliminate stretching. (Fig. 1)

Better Buttonholes

Uneven-length buttonholes or ones that don't begin and end in a straight line scream homemade. Here's how to avoid these problems:

- Make a buttonhole stitching guide. With a fabric marker and ruler, draw a buttonhole ladder on a strip of water-soluble stabilizer to use as a stitchinguide. Position guide on the garment's right side and baste. Make buttonholes, then carefully tear away the stabilizer. Use a damp cloth to dissolve away the stabilizer's residue.

- If you have a computer machine, ensure even-length buttonholes by using the automatic sliding buttonhole foot. Be sure the button is placed correctly in the foot and tightened down for the correct size.

- Puckered, out-of-shape buttonholes can be avoided with the use of tear-away stabilizer. Place a small square behind the buttonhole placement markings. Sew the buttonhole and tear away the stabilizer. Some of the stabilizer will remain under the stitching and continue to support it during wear.

- Use a cotton, machine-embroidery thread for buttonholes for a more defined look.

- Stitch in the same direction for more uniform buttonholes.

- Use the same thread in the top and bobbin for a smoother appearance.

- Loosen the upper-thread tension slightly.

- Use a new needle and the correct size for your fabric.

TIP: Use a seam sealant to clean up frayed-looking buttonholes. Trim threads and dot buttonhole beads with sealant. Always test seam sealant first on a fabric scrap to be sure it dries invisibly.

Avoid cutting through the buttonhole ends with your seam ripper by placing a straight pin at each end, just inside the stitching. The pins will help prevent you from cutting too far. If you accidentally cut too far, repair the buttonhole with a few stitches by hand and a drop of seam sealant. (Fig. 1)

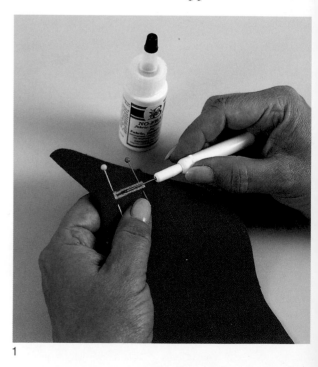

1

Use a buttonhole cutter set for more control and a neat buttonhole opening. The cutter is simply a sharp blade (like a chisel) that, with a little pressure or a slight tap of a hammer, opens the buttonhole with a clean cut. A wooden block is placed under the buttonhole to protect your working surface. (Fig. 1)

BUTTONHOLES—ON SHEERS

Sheer fabrics usually need special attention and buttonholes are no exception. Buttonholes work best when stitched horizontally, which is a more stable grain. This will keep the buttonhole from stretching out of shape with use.

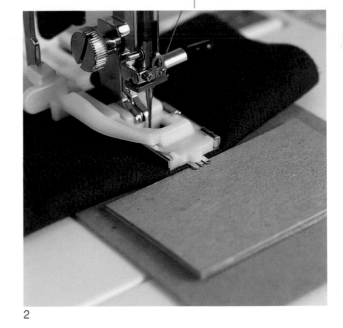

1

When stitching, it may be necessary to place a layer or two of stabilizer on the garment. Use a lightweight tear-away stabilizer on the underside or a dissolving type on the right side of the garment. (Solvy® is a dissolve-away stabilizer that when placed in water disappears.) Some stabilizers will disappear under the steam of an iron. Before stitching, it is a good idea to baste layers of stabilizer to the garment.

Try loosening the upper tension for a smooth stitch and to reduce puckering.

TIP: Use wash- or press-away stabilizer on the right side of a textured fabric so the toes of the buttonhole foot do not catch or snag the fabric loops during stitching, or, use a sliding buttonhole foot.

BUTTONHOLES— ON BULKY FABRICS

Buttonholes on jackets and coats can cause stitching difficulties due to the bulk of the center front seam. The problem is that the buttonhole foot cannot lie flat—one side of the foot is higher than the other. To help offset the difference, place a piece of cardboard under the lower side or end of the foot to level it off. With a level foot, you should be able to stitch a perfect buttonhole. (Fig. 2)

2

CREATIVE USES FOR BUTTONHOLES

Create an unusual accent on garments and home decorating items using buttonholes to weave interesting ribbons for a lacing effect. Use strips of lace, velvet, grosgrain, or satin ribbon to weave through the buttonholes, or, use bias strips of self-fabric for a decorative look.

Mark buttonhole placement using a fabric marker. For a single layer of fabric use tear-away stabilizer on the back. Make buttonholes at markings to accommodate size of ribbon/fabric being laced. Cut open and weave ribbon. If desired, add a row of decorative stitches above and below the buttonholes.

Another creative buttonhole option is to embellish a basic buttonhole with decorative stitches. Stitch a decorative pattern at the end of one buttonhole placement line. Stitch the buttonhole in place and cut it open. The decorative pattern can frame a small button or decorate a plain one. Or, before cutting the buttonhole open, surround it with decorative embroidery stitches.

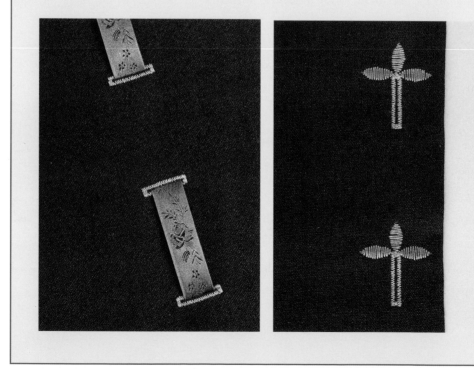

Blindhem Stitch

The blindhem stitch is used for hemming sportswear, children's clothing, and home decorating items. Blindhemming does take some practice to perfect, but stitching with a blindhem foot will help ensure invisible stitching. It works best on thicker fabrics like wools or sweatshirt fleece.

A blindhem stitch is a series of straight stitches with a zigzag that swings to the left. Most machines have a built-in blindhem stitch and a special blindhem foot to make hemming easy. Your machine also may have a stretch blindhem stitch. The straight stitches are replaced with narrow zigzag stitches designed to give with knit fabrics. (Fig. 1)

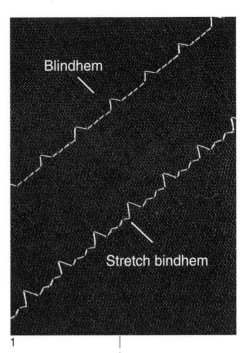

Use a stitch length of 2mm–3mm and a width setting 1mm–2mm. Loosen the top tension slightly. Press up the hem. With the garment wrong side up, fold the hem back to the right side so the cut edge extends past the fold by ¼"; pin or baste in place in place. Place the hem under the machine and guide the fold next to the blindhem foot guide. Begin stitching, making sure the straight stitches are on the extension not the fold of the garment, the zigzag should barely catch a thread in the garment's fold. Adjust the stitch width to accommodate the fabric thickness.

TIP: For blind hemming it is best to use a fine, lightweight thread and a fine needle. On thin fabrics, loosen the bobbin tension slightly, if necesary.

Beyond the Hem

Besides blind hemming, use this stitch to attach patch pockets, for appliquéing, and decorative picot edging. The blind hem foot can be used for edgestitching, topstitching, or pintucks.

— PATCH POCKETS

The blindhem stitch works to attach pockets with a hand-stitched look. Place pockets on garment and pin in place. Use matching thread and an open-toe or transparent presser foot. Use a narrow stitch width and short stitch length. Stitch with the zigzag catching a few of the pocket threads. The straight stitch should be hidden along the pocket's edge. (Fig. 2)

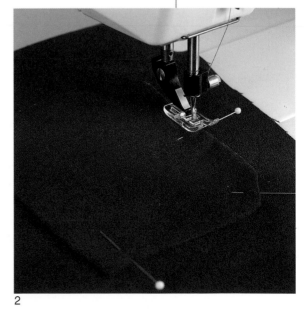

1

2

—BLINDHEM APPLIQUÉ

Try this variation of the blind hem for a hand-stitched look on appliqués. Use it in place of satin stitching. Use a clear monofilament thread in the needle for the most inconspicuous stitch. All-purpose thread can be used on the bobbin. Attach an open-toe or transparent presser foot. Decrease the stitch length to 1.5mm–2.0mm. Press under the cut edges on the appliqué or omit if fabric does not ravel (i.e. felt, synthetic suede). Pin or fuse appliqués in place. Stitch, placing the stitches so they just fall past the appliqué motif edge. (Fig. 1)

Note: This technique also will work using a blanket or buttonhole stitch for a hand-sewn look. (Fig. 2)

—PICOT EDGING

Make a picot or scalloped edge finish to hem knits and lightweight wovens. This stitch also is referred to as a shell hem and looks great on lingerie. Use the bias grain for woven fabrics and the crossgrain on knits. (Fig. 3)

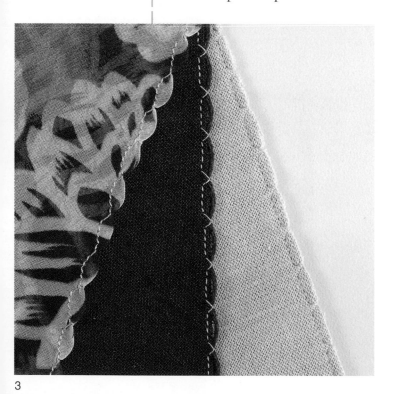

3

1

2

Attach an open-toe or transparent presser foot. Place the fold of the garment under the presser foot with the bulk to the right of the needle. Note: If your machine is computerized, use the mirror image feature to reverse the blindhem stitch. Tighten the top tension for a more pronounced scallop. Stitch, allowing the zigzag to go off the folded edge of the fabric. (Fig. 1 and 2)

To further enhance your scalloped edge place a decorative thread against the fold and incorporate within the stitch. (Fig. 3)

—MULTIPLE ZIGZAG

The multiple or triple zigzag stitch can be used for mending rips and tears. Set machine for a 3mm–5mm stitch width and 0.5mm–1mm length. Attach a satin-stitch foot. Trim any loose threads or ragged edges around the tear. Use a layer of fusible interfacing on the back side of the tear for support. Begin stitching over the tear to cover the hole.

3

GETTING
DOWN TO THE
BASICS

For larger holes use a patch and attach it with a multiple zig-zag. Cut a piece of fabric for the patch one inch larger to cover the tear or hole. Place patch on right side of garment over hole. Attach a satin-stitch foot. Stitch around the edges of the patch pivoting at the corners. (Fig. 1)

Note: Some computerized machines have sideways or lateral feeding. This eliminates the need for turning or pivoting the fabric using the built-in 4-way mending stitch. Simply press a button for the stitching direction desired.

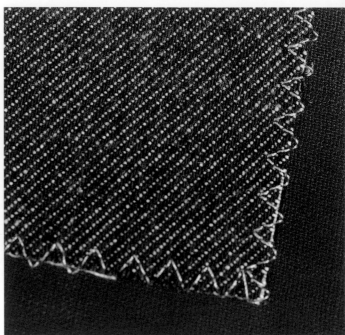

1

2

—FREE-MOTION MENDING

For very large tears or holes it will be necessary to repair them with machine darning, stitching without the presser foot or using a darning foot, an embroidery hoop, and free-motion stitching.

Remove the presser foot and lower the feed dogs. Set the stitch length at 0.5mm and width at 4mm–5mm. To keep the fabric taut while stitching without a foot, center the hole in an embroidery hoop. Place hoop under the needle and lower the presser bar to begin stitching. While holding the needle thread with one hand, draw the bobbin thread up through the fabric. Hold both thread ends and begin stitching. Move the hoop forward and backward under the needle as you stitch. Try to keep your stitching closely spaced and even. Keep the machine running at a moderate speed and move the hoop in a steady, continuous movement. (Fig. 2)

—OVEREDGE STITCH

A basic zigzag will work as an overcast to secure the edge of a ravely fabric. Many machines have built-in overedge stitch patterns that will sew a seam and overcast the fabric. You will have to trim the fabric next to the stitching for a narrow overedged seam. (Fig. 3) Consult your owner's manual for different overedge stitch options. Be sure to use the appropriate foot for best results.

SEW and EMBROIDER

EMBROIDER on TICKING

102 FLORAL ART & QUILTING DESIGNS

Rayon
COATS
DECORATIVE SEWING
46 WT.
MACHINE STITCHING
TOPSTITCHING
EMBROIDERY
USA

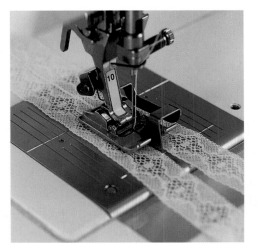

DECORATIVE STITCH OPTIONS

Today's sewing machines allow you to create a myriad of embellishments. Decorative stitch patterns are available on most every model, whether a top-of-the-line computer or a basic mechanical model. Computerized machines will allow you to combine stitch patterns, and mirror-image or reverse-image a design, and some will offer oversized patterns.

Smooth Stitching Solutions

There's no doubt most decorative stitches look more distinct with specialty threads. Before you move on to expressing your own personal style, experiment with your machine's decorative options and specialty threads on fabric scraps first. Here are a few tips for working with decorative threads.

1. Needle selection—The right needle can make all the difference in stitching success. Run a line of thread lubricant the length of the decorative thread spool. (It's not recommended for all machines—be sure to consult your dealer.) This prevents the thread from wearing away and splitting as it moves in and out of the needle's eye.

2. Tension setting—Most decorative threads are not strong and often break when stitching an intricate stitch pattern. Try reducing the tension.

3. Thread feeding—Be sure thread is not getting hung up on one of the machine's thread guides or around the spool pin. Slippery threads will feed better when placed on a vertical spool pin. Spool nets are available to help hold the thread in place.

4. Machine condition—Check the machine needle for burrs or rough spots. Is your machine due for a tune-up?

Appliqué

Appliqué offers unlimited design options for adult's and children's garments as well as home decorating items. Using the machine's zigzag stitch creates intricate appliqué patterns. Create your own designs or use purchased transfers. Other interesting patterns can be found in children's books, coloring books, and on printed fabric with floral or geometric designs. Look to appliqué pattern books for more inspiration.

HOW TO APPLIQUÉ

Fast-fuse technique—

This technique is easy because the fabric is secured to the background; fast because the cut edges will not ravel; and fabulous because the appliqué will not pucker when stitched. Plus, it will work on any fabric that can be ironed.

Begin by tracing each of the appliqué design components onto paper-backed fusible webbing. **Note:** Trace the mirror image of any asymmetrical design to prevent it from being reversed when fused to the background. (Fig. 1)

Fuse webbing to wrong side of appliqué fabrics. (Fig. 2)

Cut appliqué design from fabric following tracing. (Fig. 3)

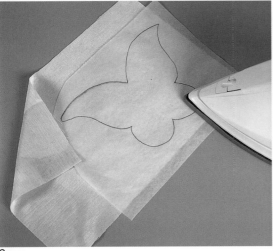

1

2

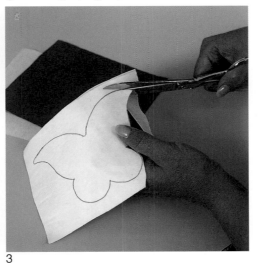

3

TIP: Create a padded appliqué by fusing a layer of batting to the underside of the appliqué fabric. Make appliqué same as instructed.

Remove paper-backing and position appliqué pieces on background. Fuse to right side of background following manufacturer's directions. Place a piece of tear-away stabilizer on underside of background to fit appliqué (this is necessary to do on knit and unstable fabrics). (Fig. 1)

 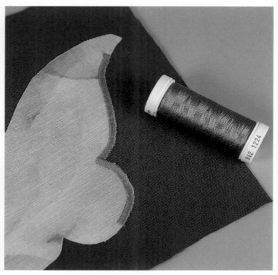

Set zigzag stitch for closely spaced stitches. Set width suitable for size of appliqué. Loosen the needle thread tension so the bobbin thread is concealed on the underside of the fabric. Satin-stitch around the appliqué. Remove any tear-away stabilizer. (Fig. 2)

1   2

Appliqué Stitching Techniques

Inside corners — Stitch past the corner the width of the satin stitching. Stop with the needle down at the inner edge of the stitching; raise presser foot and pivot. Continue stitching, covering the previous stitches at the corner. (Fig. 3)

3

Outside corners—Stitch past the corner and stop with the needle down at the outer edge of the satin stitching; raise presser foot and pivot. Continue stitching, covering the previous stitching at the corner. (Fig. 1)

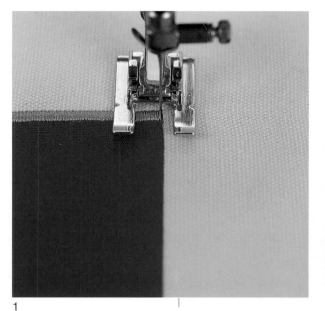

1

2

Curves—Pivot the fabric frequently with the needle down at the longest (outside) edge of the satin stitching. (Fig. 2)

Points—Tapered points are most desired since they lay down the least amount of thread for a neat point. Stitch to the point, adjusting the stitch width as you come to the point. Pivot the fabric slightly and continue stitching, gradually narrowing the stitch width to 0. Raise the presser foot; pivot fabric. Stitch over the previous stitching, gradually widening the width to its original width. (Fig. 3)

3

APPLIQUÉ BASICS

- Prewash the garment or project first and press them as needed.
- Use a photo copy machine to reduce or enlarge a particular appliqué design to fit your project.
- Follow manufacturer's instructions for all fusing products.
- Cut out all motifs before removing the fusible-web paper backing.
- Stabilize the fabric with a tear-away stabilizer placed on the wrong side and beneath the appliqué area.
- For most appliqués, use a 3mm-wide satin stitch and a length set just above 0. This can vary, so do a test sample on a fabric scrap first.
- For accents on your appliqué design, use your machine's decorative stitches.
- To lock stitches after you've completed stitching an area, set the stitch length at 0 and place 2 or 3 stitches in place.
- Keep the area to be stitched to the left of the needle. The needle swing should be to the right of the appliqué edge.

Decorative Bobbin Stitching

Thick and heavy threads that do not fit through the eye of the needle will work on the bobbin. Threads such as pearl cotton, embroidery floss, and ribbon thread can all be used in the bobbin.

To achieve this decorative effect, it is necessary to loosen the bobbin case tension. I suggest purchasing an additional bobbin case for this work so that you will always have a bobbin case ready for perfect stitching. Mark your decorative bobbin with a dab of nail polish to distinguish it from your correctly set bobbin.

A simple straight, zigzag, or feather stitch, even a star pattern, will give you special effects. Experiment with your machine's decorative stitches to see what look you desire.

For intricate designs, mark pattern on tear-away stabilizer and pin it in place on the wrong side of your garment or project. Remember, the decorative stitching is produced by the bobbin so you will need to work in reverse. Before stitching, bring up the bobbin thread to the top side and take a few stitches to prevent jamming. Stitch slowly, following markings. Remove stabilizer and pull bobbin thread to the wrong side. Knot thread ends and trim.

Silk Ribbon Embroidery

Why stitch by hand when your sewing machine can create elegant ribbon embroidery embellishments? This technique is done by drawing up silk ribbon thread to the garment's right side from a loosened bobbin. (See Decorative Bobbin Stitching.)

Use a 2mm–4mm wide silk ribbon. Hand-wind the ribbon onto a bobbin. Try to keep the ribbon as flat as possible. Loosen the bobbin case tension and thread. Be sure the ribbon pulls freely from the bobbin case with little tension. For the needle thread, use a clear monofilament or a light-color rayon thread to match. Attach an open-toe embroidery foot. Before stitching on your project, do a test sample on a fabric scrap. It may be necessary to stabilize your fabric with a lightweight iron-on interfacing. Adjust stitch length and width to achieve the desired effect. Be sure to stitch on the fabric's wrong side. After stitching, tie off and knot ribbon on the wrong side.

Satin-Stitch Scalloped Edgings

The closed or satin-stitch scallop is a series of contoured zigzag scallop stitches. Their delicate stitches beautifully finish the edges of a collar, hem, or ruffle. For a creative alternative, use a scallop stitch when appliquéing. Stitch with the points in either direction and the straight edge along the appliqué outline.

Set machine for a wide scallop stitch with a stitch length of 0.5 mm to almost 0.

Note: On computer machines most scallop stitches can be elongated or shortened for different effects. Use a transparent or metal embroidery foot. Loosen the top thread tension slightly. Use a tear-away stabilizer under the fabric to prevent puckering. Place the fabric edge so the point of the scallop catches the fabric. Half the presser foot will be on the fabric and the other half off the edge. Stitch. Remove the stabilizer carefully.

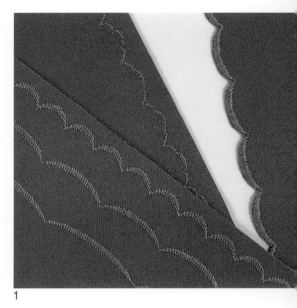
1

Dab liquid seam sealant along scallop stitching and allow to dry. With a sharp pair of scissors, cut away excess fabric close to the stitching without cutting the threads. (Fig. 1)

Corded Scallop Edge Finish

This elegant finish produces a hand-crocheted lace effect because the stitches are off-the-edge of the fabric. It is the perfect touch on collars, cuffs, and hems. Since the stitching is off the fabrics edge, cording is needed to stabilize the stitch. Use a pearl cotton thread and paper or tear-away stabilizer.

2

Set machine for a scallop satin stitch with a wide width. Attach a transparent embroidery foot for visibility. Loosen the top thread tension slightly. Place the paper or stabilizer under your fabric. Place the fabric edge so the point of the scallop catches the fabric. Half the presser foot will be on the fabric and the other half off the edge. Hold the cord while guiding the fabric with your other hand. (Fig. 2 and 3)

Remove the stabilizer carefully from the stitching.

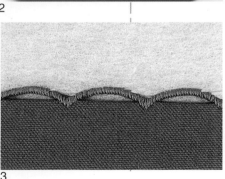
3

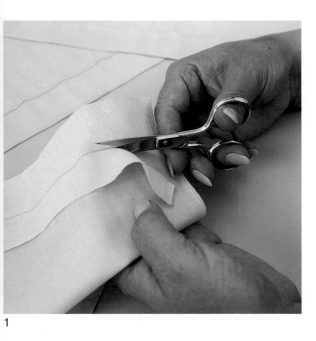

1

Straight-Stitch Scallop Border Hem

Here's a variation on the satin stitch scallop. A straight or tracery scallop is a line of straight stitches in a scallop pattern. Use it to create a shadow effect on sheer fabrics with a 2.0 or 3.0 twin needle and contrasting thread. On knit and heavier fabrics, use matching or contrasting thread and a single or twin needle.

Turn hem up and press. Set machine for a straight-stitch scallop. Attach a satin stitch or embroidery foot. Working from the right side of the fabric, stitch ½" from the cut edge of the hem. On the inside of the garment, cut the hem allowance close to the scallop stitching. I like using an appliqué scissors for a close cut. (Fig. 1)

Quilting

Use a single or twin needle and create an echo quilting effect. For twin needles, thread using decorative thread. Reduce the presser foot pressure, and using a 3.5mm stitch length (7.5 s/p/i) tighten the needle tension slightly. Quilt around a appliqué design or printed fabric motif echoing the patterns. Because the presser foot pressure is reduced, you can easily maneuver the fabric under the foot. (Fig. 2 and 3)

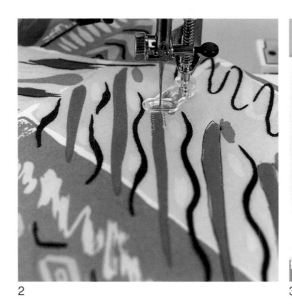

2

3

Wing Needle Stitching

A wing needle is named as such because they have "wings" or flanges on each side of the needle shaft. The wings actually poke holes in fabric for a handworked hemstitched effect. Wing needles also are referred to as hemstitch needles. Available in sizes 90/14, 100/16 and 120/20, the largest size produces the largest holes. Wing needles also are available as a double wing, featuring one wing and one standard needle on one shank. (Fig. 1) **Note:** A zigzag throat plate is required with wing needle stitching.

Traditionally a wing needle is used to create heirloom stitching on delicate or crisp woven fabrics, such as handkerchief linen, organdy, or batiste. The needle pushes the threads aside without actually breaking the threads. For the most defined effect, use a pattern that stitches in the same hole more than once. Using the bias or crosswise grain will also help produce a more open stitch. Tightening the upper tension may help to produce a more pronounced effect. For the best visibility while stitching, use an open-toe embroidery foot.

A basic zigzag stitch will create a hemstitch. For more definite holes, stitch again over the previous row of zigzag stitches making sure the needle enters the holes exactly where they were previously stitched. Many of the new computerized sewing machines feature special stitches for hemstitching. Some of my favorites are the star pattern, rickrack, picot, and pin stitches. (Fig. 2)

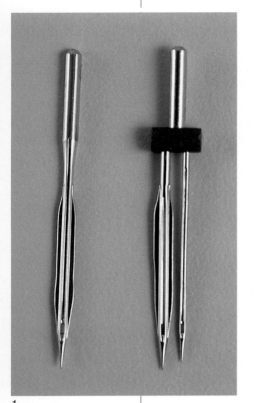

1

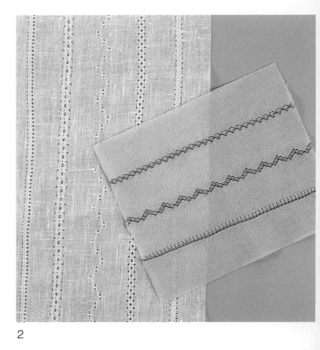

2

Lace Insertion

Straight-edged lace can be "inserted" using a wing needle within a garment rather than along the edge. Use this technique on sleeves, skirt hems, yokes and the like.

Position lace on right side of fabric, and with a straight stitch, attach lace edges to the fabric with an embroidery or satin-stitch presser foot. Turn garment over and carefully cut down the center of the fabric behind the lace. Press each cut edge back along the stitching line. With a wing needle, hemstitch close to the fold so the stitch goes just over the fold and into the lace. Cut away any excess fabric from the back side. (Fig. 1)

1

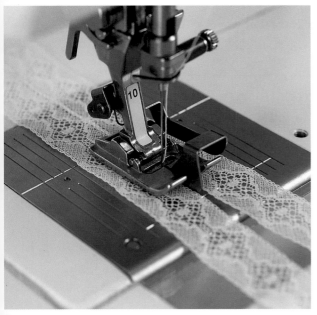

2

Joining Lace

Two straight-edged lace pieces can be joined with the hemstitching technique. Using a wing needle and an open-toe embroidery foot or edgestitch foot, select desired hemstitch pattern. Hemstitch between the two lace sections so that one side of the stitch goes over one heading and the other side goes over the other lace heading, joining the two strips. (Fig. 2)

Attaching Lace with a Double-Wing Needle

Select a straight stitch with a 1.8mm–3mm length. Use a satin-stitch foot or open-toe embroidery foot. Mark stitching line with fabric marker. Place straight edge of lace along marking. Stitch using a straight stitch with the standard needle stitching the edge of the lace and having the wing needle stitching the fabric only. Turn fabric at end of stitching. Insert needle into fabric again, just as you did previously, making sure the wing needle enters the holes at exactly the same position. **Note:** Use this same technique to add a lace accent when stitching a hem.

1

Raised Pintuck

This technique works best on fine fabrics, but you can make raised pintucks on heavier fabrics using a larger twin needle and the appropriate pintuck foot. Check with your sewing machine dealer for the correct pintuck foot for your machine and needle.

Tighten the top tension to create the "tuck". Select a straight stitch with a 2.5mm–3mm length. Attach a pintuck foot. Mark stitching lines on garment or press a crease in the fabric and use it as a starting point. For multiple rows of pintucks, continue stitching, guiding the previous tuck under one of the channels in the pintuck foot. Stitch all pintucks in the same direction. (Fig. 1)

Twin-needle and pintuck foot guide	
Needle	**Foot**
1.6mm	7- or 9-groove
2mm	7-groove
2.5mm, 3mm	5-groove
4mm, 6mm	3-groove

1

2

Fagotting

Joining two pieces of fabric with an open, lacey apprearance, faggoting looks great as a pocket or collar accent, and as a sleeve hem on a blouse. Or, use it to decorate bed sheets and other home decorating items.

Select a feather stitch, honeycomb, cross stitches, multiple-zigzag, block stitch, or hemstitch. Try different stitches on your machine to see what looks good. (Fig. 1)

Attach an open-toe embroidery foot for visibility. Or, use a pintuck foot to help maintain a uniform distance between the two fabric edges. Loosen the needle thread tension so the bobbin thread does not show on the right side of the fabric. Choose a light- to medium-weight fabric with body. Use the widest stitch width setting and a 1.5mm–2.5mm stitch length. Press under 1" on 2 fabric sections. Place the pressed edges parallel to each other about ⅛" apart. Begin stitching so that the needle goes into each edge and across the open space between the 2 fabrics. (Fig. 2)

DECORATIVE
STITCH
OPTIONS

When creating a fagotting stitch, if you are finding it difficult keeping a consistent space between the 2 fabrics, try drawing two parallel lines on a piece of paper ⅛" apart. Place the pressed edges of the fabric along the markings and hold in place with transparent tape. Your sewing machine needle will not get gummy stitching through transparent tape. (Fig. 1)

1

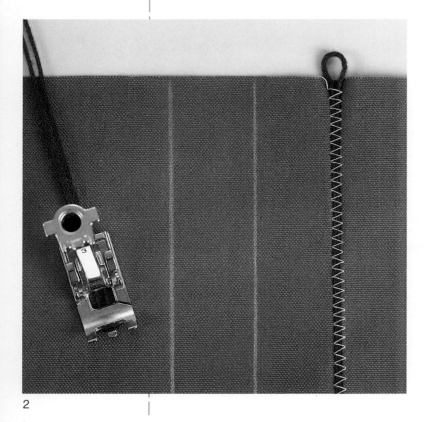

2

Smocking

Create mock-smocking on your sewing machine. Use pearl cotton and a decorative stitch for added interest.

Using a fabric marker, draw straight parallel lines to ensure even rows of smocking. Measure length of pearl cotton, twice as long as the finished smocked area. Using a standard buttonhole foot, loop the cord around the finger at the back or front of the presser foot. Select a decorative stitch and sew over both lengths of cord. To gather up fabric for smocking effect, draw up on the cord by pulling both ends. (Fig. 2)

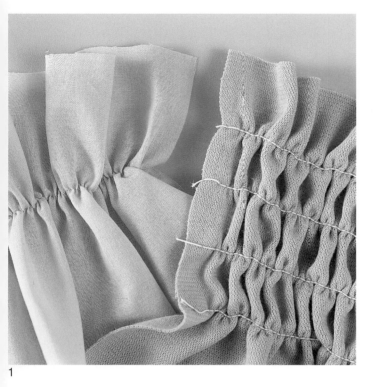

1

Smocking with Elastic Thread

This technique is used to add dimension and shape to a garment. When elastic thread is used in the sewing machine bobbin a smocking effect can be created in relatively no time. (Fig. 1)

Select a light- to medium-weight fabric. Hand-wind elastic thread onto a bobbin, being careful not to stretch the elastic. Thread bobbin as usual. Insert a standard sewing machine needle. Select a straight stitch with a 2.5mm–3mm length. Or, use a medium width, medium-length zigzag or honeycomb stitch (often called a smocking stitch). Mark stitching rows on the fabrics right side. Use a quilting guide for straight rows of stitching. (Fig. 2) Do a test sample and loosen the needle tension, if needed. Continue stitching stretching the fabric flat in front of and behind the needle as you stitch to prevent puckers. **Note:** It also may be necessary to loosen the bobbin tension for more stretch on the elastic.

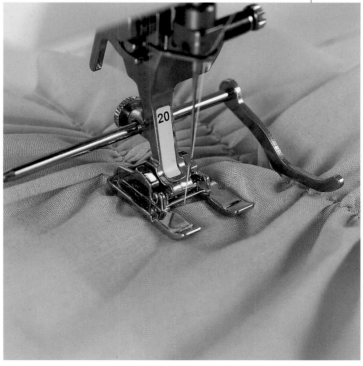

2

Passepoil. Passepoilvoet.
Passpoalfot. Passpoalfot.

⑥

Braid/Cord foot. Kordelfuß. Pied ganseur. Koordvoet. Pie
idones. Piedino per ricamare con cordoncino, Snoddfot.
09-45 ① ② ③ ④ ⑤ ⑥

Hemmer. S
Dobladillado
Päärmäysjalka
412 01 76-45

Ruffler Attachment

This accessory is just the thing for curtains, pillows and other projects that require individually adjustable gathering-effects made by small tucks.

...ring Foot

You'll find ... foot is pe... for sewing ... in very li... fabrics. It's ... a variety of hom... decor projects

Regular Sewing Foot

Having a handy extra sewing foot around for standard work is always helpful for those who sew quite a bit

SPECIAL PRESSER FEET AND ACCESSORIES

Depending on the type of sewing you do, there are various sewing machine feet and accessories available. Some of the feet listed here may come with your machine, others can be purchased separately. I have listed the accessories that are most common. Each one has a special purpose designed to save you time; others are useful when working with tricky fabrics but all will give you more professional results. Use this list to discover which feet and attachments will be the best investment for you.

SPECIAL
PRESSER FEET
AND
ACCESSORIES

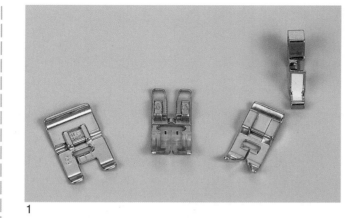

1

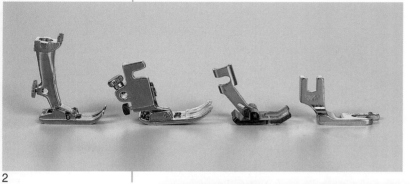

2

The Important Feet

Many of the feet listed are interchangeable. Generic feet are available for most machines and will generally save you money. Before purchasing any generic feet be sure you know the type of foot that will fit your machine. The shank is where the foot screws in or is snapped on the presser bar. Presser foot shanks can be low, high, higher or slanted. (Fig. 1 and 2) Adapters are available to fit high shank machines so they can accommodate a low shank foot. Other adapters are available for unique feet. Check with your sewing machine dealer for availability.

The bias binder — Used to apply purchased or self-fabric bias binding to a cut edge. (Fig. 3)

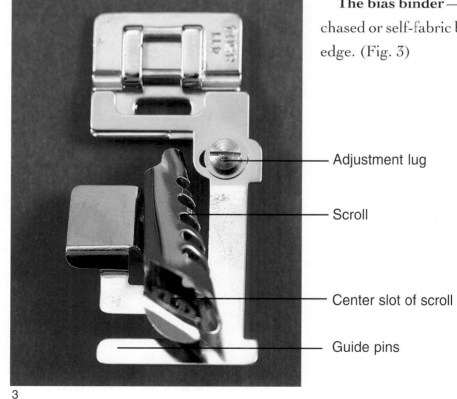

Adjustment lug

Scroll

Center slot of scroll

Guide pins

3

Cut binding diagonally and insert into the center slot of the binder. Pull binding through the scroll until it's under the needle. Lower the foot and begin stitching close to the open edge of the binding, moving the scroll to the right or left to position stitching. Do not pull the binding as it feeds through the scroll. Insert the cut edge of the fabric to be bound to the right in the center scroll as far as it will go; stitch. Use a straight or decorative stitch to attach binding. (Fig. 1 and 2)

Blindstitch foot—Used for blindhemming, this foot is excellent for topstitching. The screw on the right allows you to move the plastic adjustable guide on the foot and set the distance for topstitching where desired. (Fig. 3)

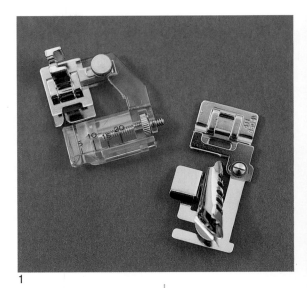

1

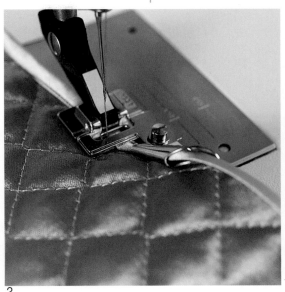

2

3

Braiding or Couching foot— Used with heavier cords, yarns, or decorative threads, this foot has aspecial hole or guide to accomodate the threads. (Fig.1)

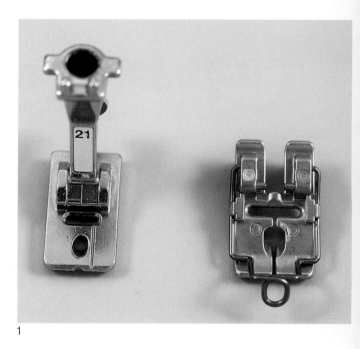

1

Circular-stitching guide—Used to stitch perfect circles, the circle maker or circular stitching devise works well with decorative embroidery stitches for novel effects. Some clip behind the presser foot like a quilting guide, and some clamp over the feed dogs, while others screw into holes in the machines bed. The circular stitcher works like a compass guiding the fabric on a pivot point for stitching a perfect circle. (Fig. 2 and 3)

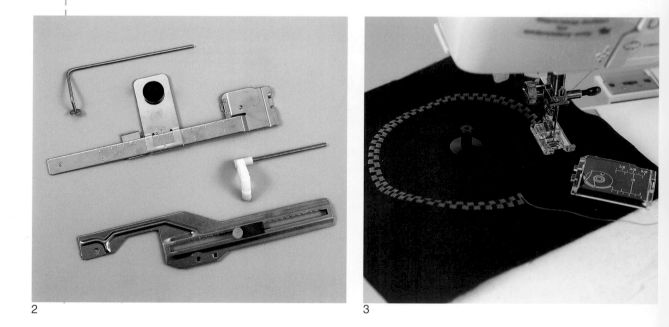

2
3

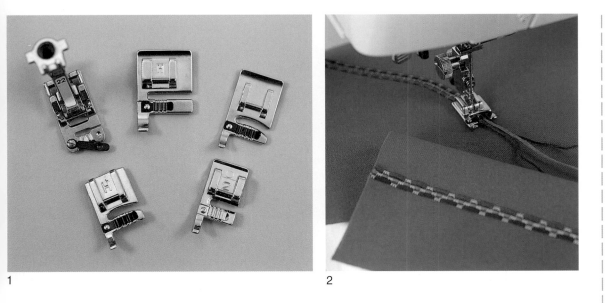

1

2

Cording foot—Single and multiple strands (5) of cord can be attached to a fabric using a cording foot. Cords are threaded through the hole in the center of the foot, then separated by the grooves on front of the foot and held in place with a clip. The cords are then held in place while stitching. Use a zigzag or decorative stitch to attach cord. (Fig. 1 and 2)

Edgestitch foot—Stitch straight stitches on the edge of a fabric. Use an edgestitch foot for hemming, edge-stitching and tucks. The foot can be adjusted with a knob or screws that moves to the right or left. Test on a fabric scrap to set proper width.

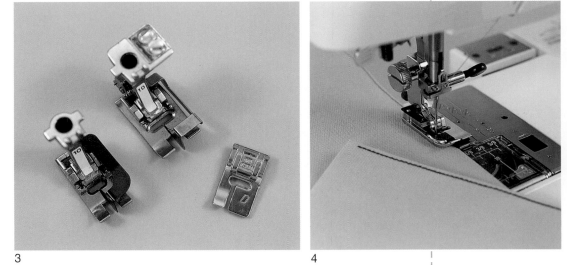

3

4

To use, fold fabric edges under and place in first slot closest to the needle. Adjust the knob to position the stitching. Stitch, guiding the fold against the edge of the slot. (Fig. 3 and 4)

Embroidery foot — This foot has a wide channel carved out of the heel on the underside of the foot. This channel allows decorative stitches to be stitched over

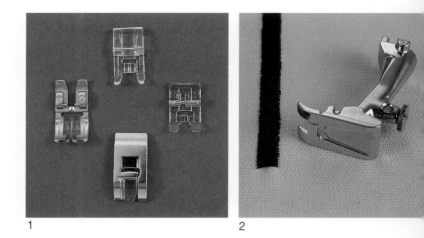

1

2

smoothly without "hanging up" on the threads and flattening them out. Available in metal and transparent plastic for greater visibility. (Fig. 1 and 2)

Eyelet plate — Eyelets are used for threading lace, cords, and ribbons, or for creating decorative effects on children's clothing and crafts. An eyelet plate fits over the feed dogs and has a short, protruding tube with an open side that allows the stitches to overcast the eyelet edge. Some machines require the feed dogs to be dropped. (Fig. 3)

3

4

5

To stitch an eyelet, set the stitch width and length to 0 (or drop the feed dogs). Place the fabric over the eyelet pin and straight-stitch around the hole to prevent it from stretching out of shape. Set the machine for a 2mm- to 6mm-wide zigzag and begin stitching, turning the fabric slowly, pivoting the work around the hole. Pull the fabric off the plate and tie off the threads. (Fig. 4 and 5)

Even-feed foot—Also called a plaid matcher, walking foot or an even-feed foot, this special foot helps feed the top layer of fabric at the same rate as the bottom layer. It works best on fabrics that stretch, creep, or slip, such as velvet, velour, or corduroy. Use it to keep stripes and plaid matched as you stitch, and for quilting, when a layer of batting is used between 2 fabrics, to keep the layers together. Some even-feed feet have quilting guides that attach for stitching straight rows. (Fig. 1 and 2)

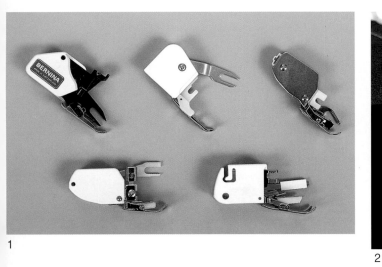

1

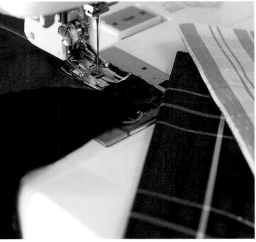

2

Felling foot—Wide-spaced toes on the foot guide fabric layers when stitching fell and flat-felled seams. It also can be used to make narrow, machine-stitched hems. (Fig. 3, 4, and 5)

3   4   5

SPECIAL
PRESSER FEET
AND
ACCESSORIES

Fringe foot—
Create self fringe
with the zigzag
or ladder stitch
and a fringe foot.
This special foot
has a raised bar
in the center. As
the needle stitches

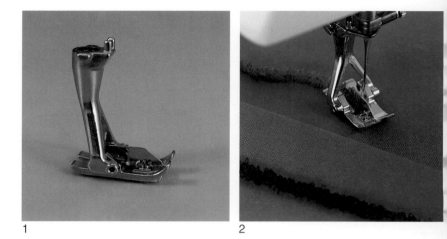

1

2

from side to side, loopy stitches form over the bar creating fringe. This foot also is used for tailor's tacks and fagotting. (Fig. 1 and 2)

Free-motion foot—Designed for free-motion stitching, this foot is also used for darning. Usually made of plastic for its transparent quality, it helps to keep the right amount of pressure on your fabric while the feed dogs are lowered. (Fig. 3 and 4)

3

4

Gathering or shirring foot — This special foot gathers or shirrs fabric as it is being stitched. Designed to gather a single layer of fabric or gather a single layer while stitching it to another fabric layer in one operation. Can be used to stitch rows of evenly spaced shirring. The gathering foot has a raised channel on the underside behind the needle position. Many also have a slot in front of the needle to gather and attach the ruffle to a flat fabric. (Fig. 1)

To use a gathering foot, set machine for a straight stitch. For fine gathers, use a short stitch and normal tension; for fuller gathers use a longer stitch length and tighten the upper thread tension. Always do a test sample first to set the stitch length where desired.

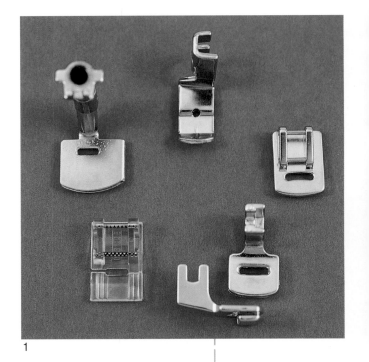

1

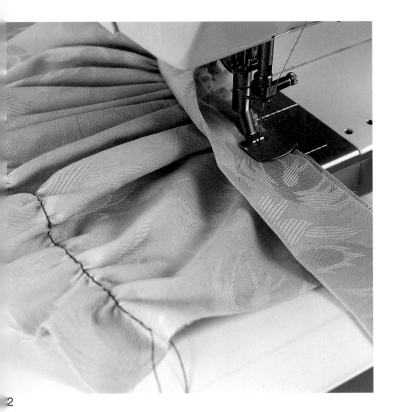

2

To gather and attach the layers simultaneously, place the fabric to be gathered under the foot, right side up. Move the needle to its left position for more control. To make rows of shirred fabric, press a crease along the crosswise grain of the fabric. Begin stitching along the crease, working out at even intervals for even spacing. Use the foot to gauge the distance of your rows of stitching. (Fig. 2)

TIP: When shirring a pocket, yoke or a garment section, shirr the fabric, then cut according to the pattern.

SPECIAL
PRESSER FEET
AND
ACCESSORIES

Hemmer foot — This scroll-type foot is designed to curl the edge of the fabric under while being stitched to form a narrow ⅛" double hem. Works best with lightweight fabrics on ruffles and scarves, or anything with long straight edges. Either straight or decorative stitches can be used. (Fig. 1)

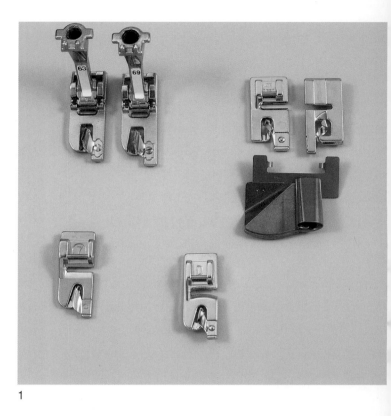

1

2

To use a hemmer foot, begin by creasing a ⅛" double hem in about 2" of the fabric's edge to be hemmed. Place the fabric under the foot and stitch through the crease for 2 or 3 stitches. It may be helpful to hold the thread ends at the back of the foot to help the fabric edge feed through the machine. Guide the fabric's edge in front to the hemmer and into the scroll. (Fig. 2)

Open-toe embroidery foot—The space between the toes of this foot is open to allow a clear view for stitching. It is particularly helpful when stitching intricate designs. Like the satin-stitch and embroidery foot, the underside has a wide channel in the

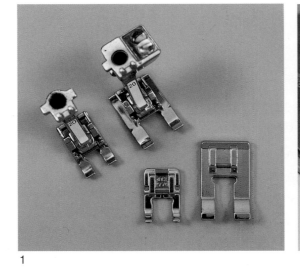

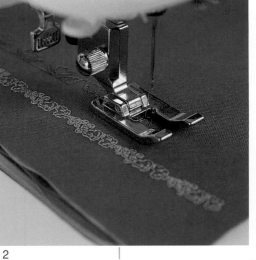

1

2

heel for gliding over decorative stitches. If an open-toe foot is not available for your machine, purchase an additional plastic satin-stitch foot and cut out the front section with a tiny saw or scissors. (Fig. 1 and 2)

Overedge or overcasting foot—Hold the fabric flat while an overedge stitch sews a seam and overcasts the cut edge of the fabric in one operation. A center metal bar or wire on the foot is designed to hold the fabric flat as it is being stitched. Works especially well on fabrics that roll, such as tricot and lightweight knits. (Fig. 3 and 4)

3

4

SPECIAL
PRESSER FEET
AND
ACCESSORIES

Pintuck foot— This foot works with a twin needle to create narrow tucks in lightweight fabric. Grooves underneath the foot keep the tucks evenly spaced. It is necessary to tighten the upper tension to accomplish this. (Fig. 1 and 2)

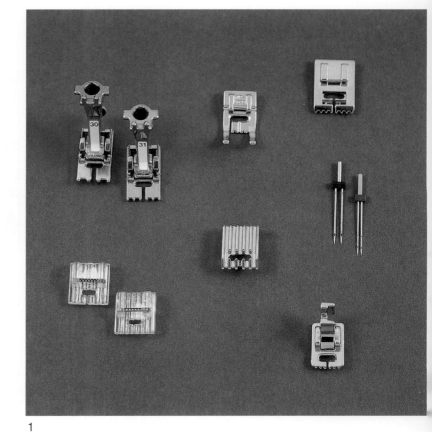

1

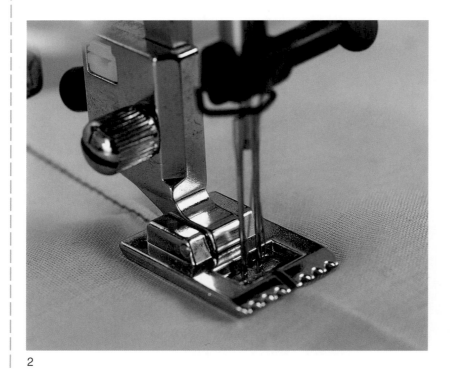

2

Quilting or patchwork foot—Designed for stitching exact ¼" seams used for piece quilting, the foot has a measure right-hand side an exact ¼" width from the needle and is used as a guide. The foot is usually marked in front and behind the center needle position for ¼" seams. The markings help when pivoting, stopping and starting. (Fig. 1 and 2)

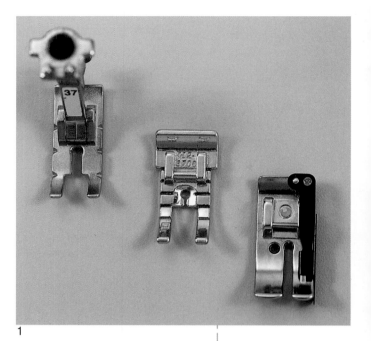

1

2

Quilting guide or edge guide—The guide is designed to help keep lines of stitching straight. Slide the adjustable rod into the opening on the back of the presser foot holder and screw in place. Stitch one row of quilting then guide the quilter over the previous row to keep lines parallel. Use it to stitch parallel to a seam. (Fig. 1 and 2)

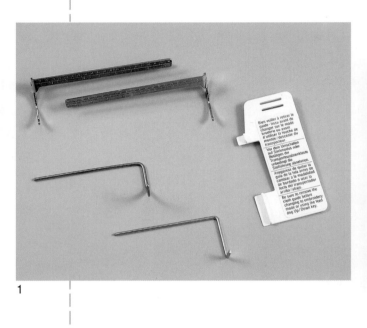

1

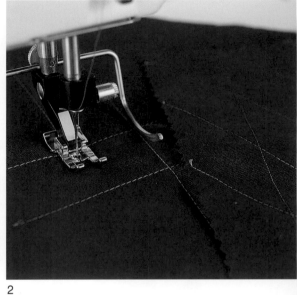

2

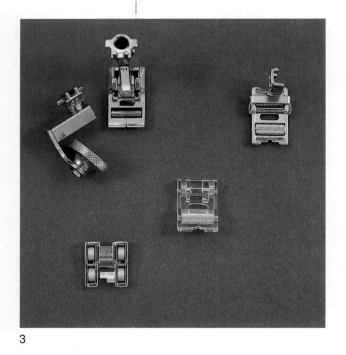

3

Roller foot—Two or more rollers are fitted into the front and back of this foot. (Fig. 3) It is used for stitching leather (Fig. 5), vinyl (Fig. 6), velvet, and slippery fabrics. A roller foot is ideal for plaid and napped fabrics when shifting occurs. Some feet have straight grooves, while others are smooth. The rollers act like another set of feed dogs that help move the fabric between the foot and feeding system, keeping them from shifting. It will allow stitches to glide over leathers and vinyls without sticking to the foot. Use a roller foot to stitch bulky outerwear fleece. (Fig. 4) When stitching slippery fabrics, use full presser foot pressure.

4   5   6

Ruffler foot — A ruffler will gather and pleat light- to medium-weight fabric. (Fig. 7)

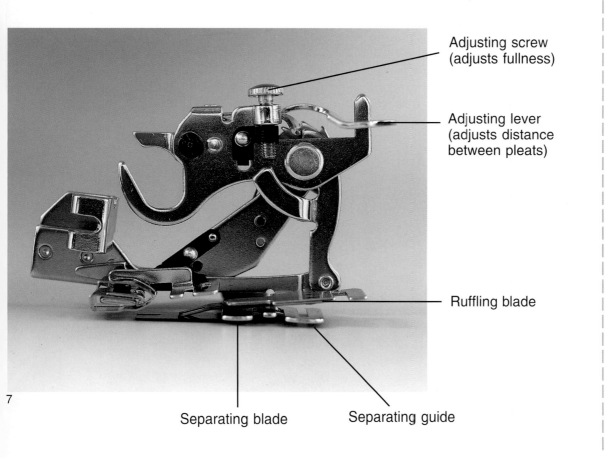

Adjusting screw
(adjusts fullness)

Adjusting lever
(adjusts distance
between pleats)

Ruffling blade

7

Separating blade   Separating guide

To ruffle fabric, cut the fabric 2 to 3 times the desired finished length. Finish the lower edges with a narrow hem or use the hemmer foot.

To gather, set the adjusting screw clockwise. Test a scrap of fabric and set stitch length for desired fullness; a short stitch produces more fullness than a long stitch. Insert fabric between 2 blades. Stitch.

To create a ruffle and attach to another fabric in one step, insert ruffle with wrong side up between the blades. Place the joining fabric right side up, between the ruffler and the feed dog, align the cut edges and stitch.

To pleat fabric, adjust ruffler having the adjustment lever set at 6 or 12 (stitches apart). Turn the adjusting screw clockwise as far as it will go. Set stitch length as desired (the shorter the stitch the closer the pleats). Insert fabric between blades and stitch. Press in pleats with an iron. (Fig. 1 and 2)

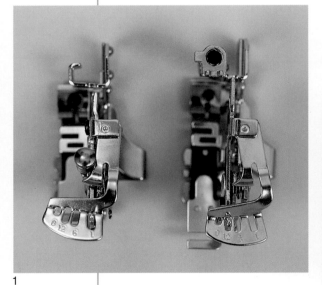

1

2

Satinedge foot— Adjustable guide and open toe allows you to create a prefect satin stitch along the edge of a fabric. (Fig. 1 and 2)

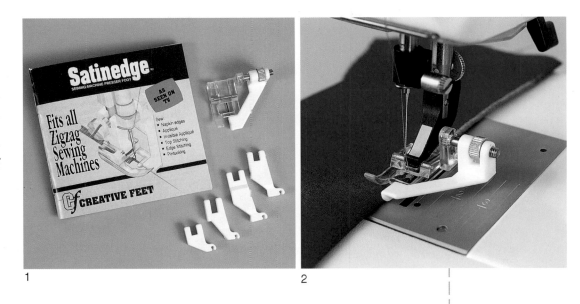

1

2

Sequins and ribbon foot— This accessory works to attach sequins by machine with a 6.5mm zigzag width. Insert ¼"-wide trim into guide which attaches to a satin-stitch foot. To attach elastic, the guide feeds elastic while the machine stitches. (Fig. 3, 4, and 5)

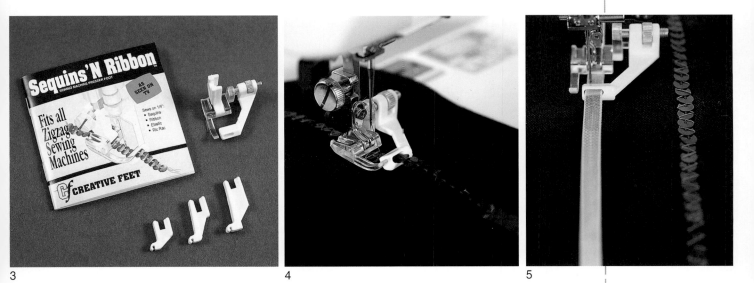

3

4

5

Side cutter—The side cutter works like a serger to cut the fabric while the machine makes overcasting stitches around the edge. It can be attached to a zigzag sewing machine. (Fig. 1 and 2)

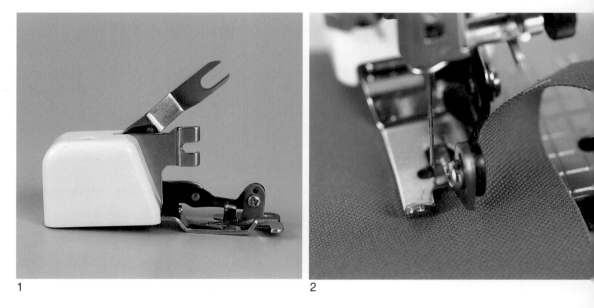

1

2

Straight-stitch foot—This foot has a narrow opening with 2 toes of different lengths and widths. The bottom is flat and the needle hole is a small round opening designed to provide support for the needle, and to eliminate puckering and skipped stitches. Use it on heavy fabrics to prevent the needle from pulling and pushing the fabric up and down with each stitch. (Fig. 3 and 4)

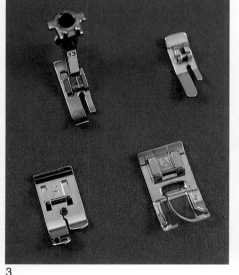

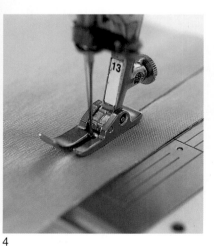

In addition to the straight-stitch foot, a straight-stitch throat plate is available with one small hole. This plate will further reduce puckering when working on fine silk and silkies, and delicate heirloom stitching. **Note:** Before stitching with a straight stitch plate, be sure the needle is centered.

3

4

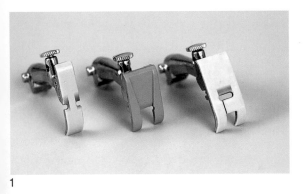

1

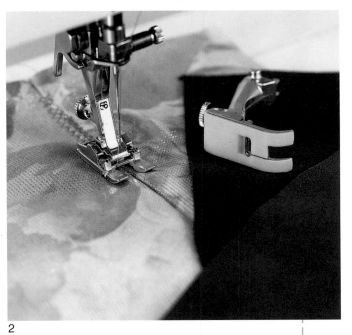

2

Teflon™ **feet** — A Teflon-coated foot is helpful in straight stitching and embroidering on leather, vinyl, suede, and other sticky fabrics. It prevents fabric from tugging and pulling against the foot. (Fig. 1 and 2)

Welting or piping foot — With a single extra-high channel on its underside, it guides ⅛" to ¼" pearls, corded piping, and welting. Use a zigzag stitch to attach trim. (Fig. 3, 4, and 5)

3

4

5

Zipper feet—It is designed to get close to the zipper teeth. Many machines have various needle positions which allows you to move the foot into position, close to the zipper teeth. Usually comes with your machine. (Fig. 1)

Also use your zipper foot for attaching a self fabric and purchased welting. To make self-fabric welting, rap cord with bias strip, right sides out, keeping cut edges even. Attach zipper foot, select a straight stitch, and adjust the needle position as needed. Stitch close to cord, but do not "crowd" the stitching against the cord. To apply welting, pin to right side of fabric, keeping line of stitching on the seamline. Move needle to the right, or closer to the cord to "crowd" it. Stitch. (Fig. 2)

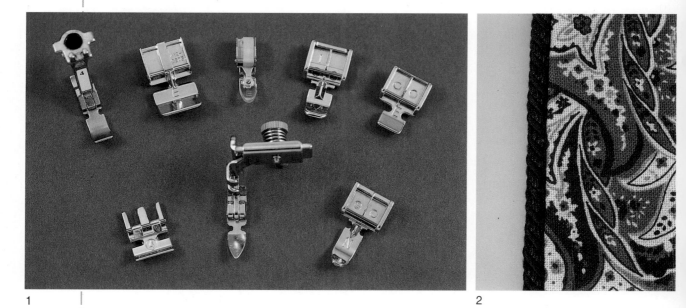

1

2

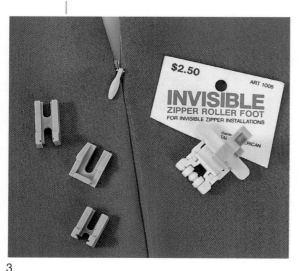

3

Invisible zipper foot—With 2 underside grooves, the invisible zipper foot rides over the zipper coil as you stitch. (Fig. 3)

Open zipper and press to uncoil. Place on half of zipper face down on the seam allowance. The tetth should be placed exactly on the seamline. Begin stitching. The coil of the zipper should run through the groove on the foot with the needle in the center of the foot. Stitch to the end of the zipper tape. (Fig. 1)

Close the zipper and position the coil, face down, on the remaining side of the seam allowance. Pin in place. Open the zipper and place the coil in the groove on the foot. Stitch. (Fig. 2)

To finish, close the zipper and complete the lower seam by moving the zipper foot to the left. Making sure the zipper is out of the way, stitch the seam. If the teeth of the zipper show on the right side when the zipper is closed, re-stitch.

Specialty Feet

Another specialty add-on item designed for decorative options is Elna Sewing Machine Company's Amazing Trace® Embroiderer. This unique attachment will fit any sewing machine brand or model and works on this premise:

Place a pattern, sketch or photo on the Amazing Trace circular pattern disc and mount it in the tray to the left of the machine. Secure fabric in the embroidery hoop portion of the attachment and insert the hoop under the machine's needle. Trace the design by moving the tray so the point of the special tracing bar follows the pattern lines. As you move the tray, your machine will echo your movements using a straight or zigzag stitch.

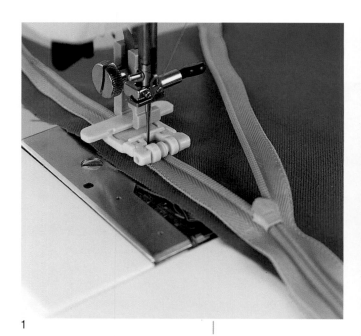

1

2

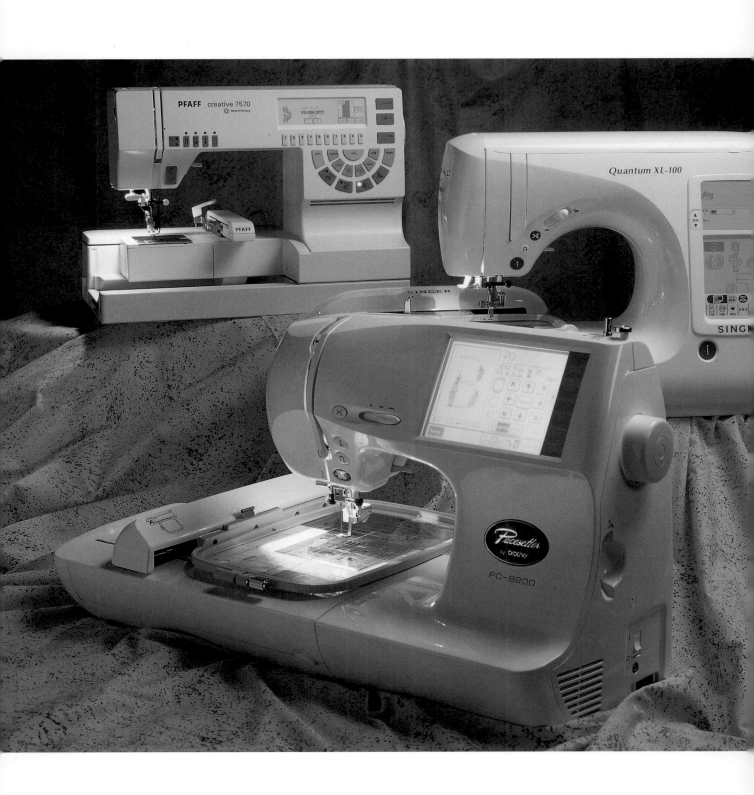

COMPUTER TECHNOLOGY IN THE SEWING ROOM

Computerized sewing machines have come a long way since the first models were introduced. Thanks to impressive technological strides, sewing machines allow the homesewer to create intricate embroidered motifs, lacy edgings, professional-looking monograms and a host of other effects with little more than a touch of a button.

Computer Sewing Machines

Computer-operated machines have the capabilities to combine up to 35 (some can do more) built-in stitches and store those stitches in one or more permanent memories to be called up later on. Any pattern can be adjusted to suit your needs: change the stitch density; enlarge, reduce or elongate a pattern; create a mirror image; or rotate a design 90° to 360° for perfect placement.

Best of all, today's computer machines can be updated with design disks, cards, cassettes, or a drawing option, making their long-term potential even more impressive. These updatable disks often contain as many as 35 embroidery designs. Motifs can be stitched up to 5" in size much like those produced by professional-embroidery machines. Choose from a wide variety of designs such as holiday, sports, juvenile, kitchen, sewing motifs, and more.

Trace-and-touch sewing is another design-expanding option. Some sewing machine companies offer this creative choice that lets you draw a design on grid paper, then program the points and enter them into your sewing machine. View your original designs on the machine's display screen. Some machines allow you to combine original designs with built-in stitches and store them in the machine's memory.

Embroidery-only machines

Sewing machine technology has made way for another type of unique machine specializing in large-size embroidery. Thanks to the latest generation of programmable sewing machines, professional machine embroidery can be done with a touch of a button. These machines do not sew a straight stitch; they do however, create intricate embroidered motifs that rival the best commercial embroidery machines.

These machines work similarly to many of today's top-of-the-line computer models with a computer-guided hoop that attaches to a movable bed that stitches forward, backward, and side-to-side with fabric manipulation. Manufacturers have built-in features to guide you step-by-step through the operations process with on-screen instructions. With a touch of a button the screen will view and check each pattern selected before stitching. An edit function allows you to adjust stitch density and enlarge or reduce patterns as desired. When it's time to change the thread color for a multicolored design, the machine stops and signals you. Thread the needle with the next color, press "start", and the machine continues to stitch the design.

Multicolored designs and monograms are sized up to 4" x 6". Choose from a complete selection of built-in stitches, including an alphabet in 3 sizes and frame patterns in various designs. Store stitch combinations in the machine's permanent memory for retrieval later on. Like computer sewing machines, these models can be updated with the same design cards or discs and work with scanned original designs.

The Scanner

A separate scanning device is now available to the homesewer for designing and creating your own stitch patterns, by scanning images onto design or memory cards that can be inserted into a computer sewing machine and embroidery-only machines.

Technically, a scanner transforms images into digital data that can be manipulated by a computer. The image can be any traceable design from a simple sketch to a fabric print. Today, hand-held versions of sophisticated computer scanners are available to the

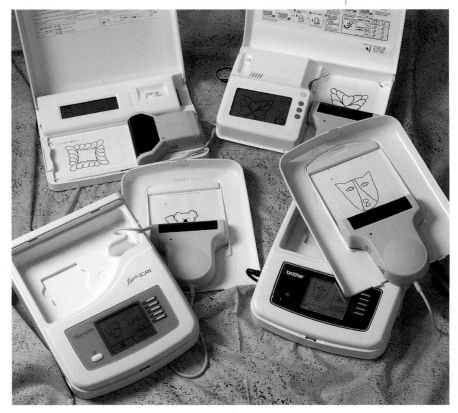

homesewer. Best of all, you don't have to be a computer technician to set up a hand-held scanner. They are simple to install and just like the sewing machine, most models have LCD screens that prompt your through the scanning and stitching process.

Using these scanners begins by using the special marker to trace or draw a design onto the tracing paper provided with the unit. The traced design is placed into a guide on the scanner's board so the scanning device can then be passed over the design for copying. The image is then saved on a blank design or memory card which is inserted into the sewing machine for stitching.

Creating multicolor designs is done in stages by tracing only portions of the design at a time. This involves using the marker to blacken in everything to be filled in as a color. Each new color requires a separate scan.

Once the image is scanned, it can be altered to further individualize it. Enlarge or reduce it; change the stitch density; choose a border outline or leave it with fill stitches only; rotate the image up, down or from side to side; add letters or numbers. Most scanners have two-card capability which allows you to mix images with those from the manufacturer's design cards to further personalize a motif.

Use a scanner to:

- Copy a print fabric and stitch it out on a coordinating fabric to make accessories.
- Embroider original slogans and logos onto items.
- Copy the pattern of your china to embroider matching tablecloths and napkins.
- Create original logos for your business.
- Scan your signature to personalize items

The PC in the sewing room—Get connected

As we all become more computer literate, sewing machine companies have created a link that hooks up your personal computer with your sewing machine. Using specially designed software allows you to create elaborate original designs right on the computer screen then stitch it out on your sewing machine.

Using the computer's mouse as a paintbrush and the screen as your canvas, create original designs. Fill, rotate, enlarge or reduce the design as desired. Further customize your designs with scanning options. Store your computerized designs on a programmable card, use the special reader/writer unit, then insert into the machine.

Special software that is installed on your computer lets you design your own decorative and embroidery stitches. You can even use computer clipart or scanned images from other graphics programs.

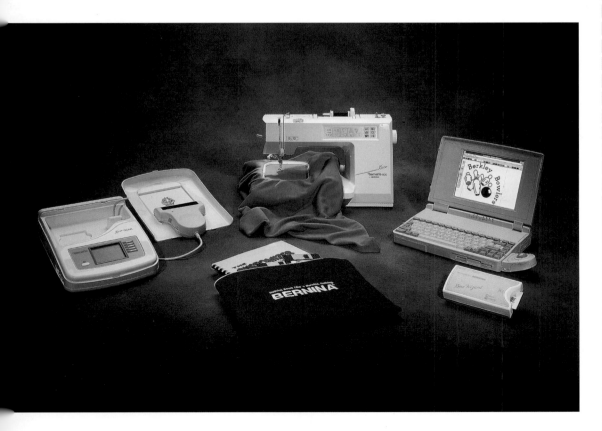

Beseler Du...
• The all-purpose
  removes micros...
• Completely dry;
  instruments, neo...
  lenses, electronic...
  (Do not use on ca...
  or on plastic body...
• Non-flammable.

Spray Nozzle Can
Hold can upright, six...
Use trigger to adjust s...
short, even bursts. F...
places, simply attach...

SINGER
SEWING MACHINE
OIL

SINGER SEWING MACHINE COMPANY

25

FIG. 25. END VIEW, SHOWING OILING POINTS

E1276B

Take out the face plate thumb screw (B, Fig. 24)
and remove the face plate. Put one drop of oil into
each of the oil holes and joints thus uncovered, as
indicated in Fig. 25, then replace the face plate and
thumb screw.

To Oil the Hook Mechanism, occasionally apply
a drop of oil at the hook bearing indicated by B,
in Fig. 11.

CARING FOR YOUR MACHINE

Regular cleaning will prevent many sewing problems and help to extend the life of your machine. Many of the newer models are self-oiling but still may require periodic oiling in the bobbin area. Consult your owner's manual for oiling points. Be sure to use sewing machine oil only, not ordinary household oil (like WD-40), it's too heavy for your sewing machine's delicate parts.

TIP: Don't use the thin plastic cover that comes with your sewing machine. These covers tends to cause the machine to sweat and corrode, especially if your machine is kept under or close to a window.

Care And Maintenance

With proper care and maintenance, a sewing machine should be checked and retimed with average use, once a year. Some machine manufacturers suggest scheduling a routine dealer maintenance. Keeping your machine clean and properly oiled (if recommended) will keep it running for years. It helps maintain high-quality stitching and avoids costly repairs. Lint in the bobbin and in the upper tension are the primary reasons for tension inconsistencies. A well cared for machine will require less maintenance than one that is neglected.

When your machine is having stitching problems and everything you try fails, it's time for professional help. Try, if you can, to leave the machine set as it was when the stitching snafu occurred. Take a sample of the stitching on the fabric you were working on to the dealers store. This will help the repair person understand what is wrong.

Before You Begin

It is always a good idea before you begin any sewing project to clean your machine. So, the more you sew, the more often you need to clean your machine. Follow these guidelines for a smooth running machine:

- Clean lint from your machine after every project sewn.
- Change the needle after every project or garment.
- Oil the machine after every 15–20 hours. Be careful not to over-oil the motor; 1 or 2 drops twice a year is enough. Note: It is always a good idea to check your owner's manual before oiling your machine. Not all machines require oil. Computerized models don't; neither do machines with oil permanently embedded in them.

To remove lint use a brush or a small vacuum cleaner attachment. Canned air is not recommended by most machine manufacturers. You can blow dirt back into the machine.

Basic Machine Maintenance is a Must

Unplug your machine and remove the needle and presser foot. Consult your owner's manual for oiling points. Occasionally clean between the tension disks with a soft, lint-free fabric. Check the needle plate for burrs and rough spots, these may need to be taken care of by a professional repair person. After cleaning, insert a new needle.

On computerized machines with front-load bobbins, remove the bobbin case and, if possible, the race cover and hook; dust out the lint. Oil if required in your owner's manual. Replace the race cover, hook, and bobbin case. (Fig. 2)

TIP: Use your hair blow dryer set on cool to blow out dust in your bobbin case. Use a clean mascara brush to dust hard-to-reach places in your sewing machine.

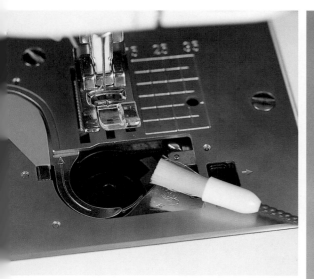

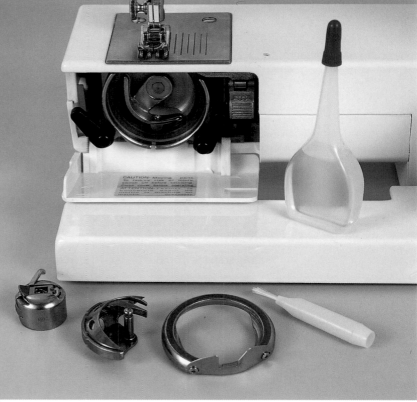

2

For top-load bobbins, remove the bobbin and dust out the lint. (Fig. 1)

With mechanical machines, clean the bobbin case as instructed for computerized machines. Also, remove the machine's upper cover, move the handwheel by hand and place a drop of machine oil anywhere metal moves against metal. Caution: Do not oil nylon gears.

147

If your machine is a flatbed, tip it back in the case or cabinet and oil spots where metal moves against metal.

Before inserting a new needle and bobbin, plug machine in and run at full speed for a few minutes to give the oil a chance to work into the parts.

MAINTENANCE DO'S AND DON'TS

- Do use a new needle with every new project.
- Do take owners lessons to learn proper maintenance techniques from your sewing machine dealer.
- Do take your machine into an authorized dealer once a year for a tune up and cleaning.
- Don't lubricate computerized machines.
- Don't use household oil on your machine. Do use sewing machine oil.
- Don't stitch with bargain thread. This causes lint build-up and inconsistent thread tension.
- Don't use inexpensive needles which cause skipped stitches.
- Don't blow out dust and lint with your breath. The moisture in your breath can harm the machine.

Helpful Cleaning Tools and Notions

Lint brush removes lint from the machine's race. Extra-fine bristles work well to remove the finest lint. Check camera and computer stores for brushes.

Canned air is a dry, clean, ozone-safe product that removes dust without leaving residue.

Mini-vacuum attachment sets are available for cleaning your machine. They attach to your vacuum cleaner to suck out lint and dust in hard to reach places. A special adapter attaches to the hose end of any vacuum cleaner.

Zoom-spout® is a telescoping spout affixed to sewing machine oil. It is used to oil hard-to-reach places.

IMPORTANT TERMS TO KNOW

Hook — The shuttle movement that determines how the machine forms a stitch.

Hook-race cover — The plate that holds the shuttle in the race. On many machines, it can be opened and the shuttle removed for oiling the race.

Race — The circular track in which the shuttle operates.

Shuttle — The moving holder that carries the bobbin thread as it "hooks" the needle thread to form a lockstitch.

Troubleshooting Guide

For each situation there is usually more than one probable cause. So keep your frustration in check as you go through each step.

1. **Uneven stitching**—Could be a tension problem. Do a tension test by running a row of stitching on the bias of the fabric. Now, pull on the fabric until the thread breaks. If the needle thread breaks, loosen the top tension. If the bobbin thread breaks, tighten the top tension.

2. **Skipped stitches**—Check the needle. Is it inserted correctly? Try a different size needle size and type (see charts on pages 43 and 45) one that may work better for your fabric. Have a selection of varying needles on hand for this purpose.

3. **Slanted stitching**—If your stitches seem to lean in one direction try stitching in different directions on a fabric scrap. Does the fabric's grain affect the look of the stitch?

4. **When beginning a seam, the fabric is being sucked down into the machine's needle plate**—Loosely woven, lightweight, and silky fabrics tend to do this. Try increasing the presser foot pressure and use a smaller needle size. If your machine has a straight-stitch needle plate (one with a single hole for the needle) use it. If necessary, hold the thread tails slightly taut and to the side of the foot when beginning to stitch so the feed dogs can do their job. Or, use a scrap of tear-away stabilizer to give your seam a place to start. Begin stitching through the stabilizer and then onto your fabric.

5. **Wavy seams**—This will happen when the stitches are too small for the fabric. Correct this by lengthening the stitch.

6. **Puckered seams**—Check the tension again. A seam will pucker if the tension are too tight. If this doesn't help, try decreasing the presser foot pressure, using a finer needle, a different presser foot, and/or a shorter stitch length.

7. **Thread loops form on underside** — Tighten the needle tension. Check the needle. Make sure the thread in the needle and bobbin are the same weight.

8. **Thread jams** — Is the presser foot lowered? Make sure the presser foot screw that holds it in place is securely tightened. Before lowering foot, bring the thread tails under the foot and to the back or side of the machine.

9. **Top thread breaks** — Try rethreading the machine, adjust the tension and check the needle. Are the top and bottom threads compatible? Another possible cause is a burr on the needle plate. This can happen after a needle has been deflected off the plate and broken while stitching. To remove the burr, use an emery cloth (not sand paper) to gently file the rough spot.

10. **Bottom thread breaks** — Clean the bobbin case and rethread the bobbin.

11. **Needle breaks** — Check to be sure the needle is inserted correctly and the needle clamp is screwed on tight. Check the top tension and needle size. A too fine needle for your fabric will cause the needle to break. Are you pulling or pushing the fabric through the machine as it is stitching with your hands, causing strain on the needle? Let the machine's feed dogs do the work.

TIP: Thread lubricants will minimizes friction between the thread and the metal parts on sewing machines helping to eliminate thread breakage, shredding and skipped stitches. A word of caution: Thread lubricants are not recommended for all machines. Some machine manufacturers claim some lubricants deposit damaging residues on the machine's moving parts. Check with your sewing machine dealer before using any thread lubricant on your machine.

BIBLIOGRAPHY

The Complete Book of Sewing Shortcuts, Claire B. Shaeffer, Sterling
   Publishing Co., Inc. NY, 1981.

Complete Guide to Sewing, Reader's Digest, The Reader's Digest
   Association, Pleasantville, NY,

The Encyclopedia of Sewing Techniques, Jan Eaton, Barron's,
   Woodbury, NY, 1986

Fine Machine Sewing, Carol Laflin Ahles, The Taunton Press,
   Newtown, CT, 1996.

Sewing Essentials, Singer Sewing Reference Library, Cy DeCosse
   Incorporated, Minnetonka, MN, 1984

A Step-by-Step Guide to Your Sewing Machine, Jan Saunders,
   Chilton Book Company, Radnor, PA, 1990.

A special thank you to the following companies:

Clotilde
2 Sew Smart Way
B8031
Stevens Point, WI 54481-8031
(800) 772-2891

Nancy's Notions
33 Beichl Ave.
P.O. Box 683
Beaver Dam, WI 53916-0683
(800) 833-0690

The Sewing Room
1274 E. Chicago Ave
Naperville, IL 60540

Speed Stitch
3113 Broadpoint Dr.
Harbor Heights, FL 33983
(800) 874-4115

Perfect Posture from Body-Rite Posture Pleaser
Box 599
Belton, TX 76513
(800) 490-7483

Sewing Machine Companies

For information on the latest machine models and/or to
locate an authorized dealer nearest you:

Allyn International
Necchi Sewing Machines
1075 Santa Fe Dr.
Denver, CO 80204
(800) 825-9987

Baby Lock U.S.A.
1760 Gilsinn La.
Fenton, MO 63026
(800) 433-2952

Bernina of America
Bernina and Bernette Sewing Machines
3500 Thayer Ct.
Aurora, IL 60504-6182
(800) 405-2Sew

Brother International
200 Cottontail La.
Somerset, NJ 08875-6714
(800) 42- Brother

Elna, Inc.
1760 Gilsinn La.
Fenton, MO 63026
(800) 848- Elna

Sears
Kenmore Sewing Machines
JAMAC, Inc.1822 Brummel Dr.
Elk Grove, IL 60007
(847) 758-0900

Janome-New Home Sewing Machine
Company
10 Industrial Ave.
Mahwah, NJ 07430
(800) 631-0183

Pfaff American Sales Corporation
610 Winters Ave.
Paramus, NJ 07653
(800) 99-Pfaff

Riccar of America
1760 Gilsinn La.
Fenton, MO 63026
(314) 349-3000

Singer Sewing Company
4500 Singer Rd.
Murfreasboro, TN 37130
(800) 877-7762

Husqvarna Viking
11760 Berea Rd.
Cleveland, OH 44111
(216) 252-3311

White Sewing Machine Company
11760 Berea Rd.
Cleveland, OH 44111
(216) 252-3311

Most sewing machine companies have web sites available for your easy reference.

ABOUT THE AUTHOR

 Karen is a magazine writer and book editor who specializes in sewing, home decorating and crafts. Having been corporate education manager for The McCall Pattern Company, an educational consultant for several sewing machine and related industries, she began free lancing in 1992. Since then her work has appeared in *McCall's Pattern Magazine, Sew News, Family Circle, What's New In Home Economics, Sewing Decor and Vogue & Butterick's Home Decorating Projects* book. Most recently she compiled and edited *The Experts Book of Sewing Tips and Techniques*. Her latest book *Fun Fast Fusible: NoSew Crafting* is a Sterling/Sewing Information Resources project.

Ms. Kunkel is the host of "Karen's Craft Corner" which can be seen on an ABC affiliate network in Albany, NY twice monthly. She demonstrates the pleasures of crafts with quick and easy projects for all ages. She also has appeared on Home Shopping Network demonstrating sewing machines and sergers.

A graduate with a B.A. in Home Economics from Plattsburgh State University in New York, Karen has been fortunate to turn her hobby into a career.

METRIC CONVERSION CHART

Yards	Inches	Meters
1/8	4.5	0.11
1/4	9	0.23
3/8	13.5	0.34
1/2	18	0.46
5/8	22.5	0.57
3/4	27	0.69
7/8	31.5	0.80
1	36	0.91
1 1/8	40.5	1.03
1 1/4	45	1.14
1 3/8	49.5	1.26
1 1/2	54	1.37
1 5/8	58.5	1.49
1 3/4	63	1.60
1 7/8	67.5	1.71
2	72	1.83

METRIC EQUIVALENTS

INCHES TO MILLIMETERS AND CENTIMETERS
MM—millimeters   CM—centimeters

Inches	MM	CM	Inches	CM	Inches	CM
1/8	3	0.3	9	22.9	30	76.2
1/4	6	0.6	10	25.4	31	78.7
3/8	10	1.0	11	27.9	32	81.3
1/2	13	1.3	12	30.5	33	83.8
5/8	16	1.6	13	33.0	34	86.4
3/4	19	1.9	14	35.6	35	88.9
7/8	22	2.2	15	38.1	36	91.4
1	25	2.5	16	40.6	37	94.0
1 1/4	32	3.2	17	43.2	38	96.5
1 1/2	38	3.8	18	45.7	39	99.1
1 3/4	44	4.4	19	48.3	40	101.6
2	51	5.1	20	50.8	41	104.1
2 1/2	64	6.4	21	53.3	42	106.7
3	76	7.6	22	55.9	43	109.2
3 1/2	89	8.9	23	58.4	44	111.8
4	102	10.2	24	61.0	45	114.3
4 1/2	114	11.4	25	63.5	46	116.8
5	127	12.7	26	66.0	47	119.4
6	152	15.2	27	68.6	48	121.9
7	178	17.8	28	71.1	49	124.5
8	203	20.3	29	73.7	50	127.0